Equally Insignificant

Andy Hutchinson

The Wishing Well *Publishers*

Author's Note

All characters in this book, with the exception of Lanna Green, are loosely based on real people but in most instances names have been changed. Events described in this book are for the most part fictitious, or at the very least exaggerated out of all proportion to the actual events that they are based on. None of the characters in this book - with the sole exception of Billy Hunt's reference character - ever broke the law or acted without good faith in the context of any event described in this book or any promotional material associated with this book. BP, ICI and Fina are real companies but any negative portrayal of their business practices and conduct is entirely fictitious. All are believed by the author to be excellent employers and all work within their spheres of influence in the finest traditions of their good name and reputation. The author would like to thank Sarah Stocks for her continued guidance in all the above related matters but it must be made clear that she is in no way responsible for any lapse in adherence to that guidance as given.

Copyright © Andy Hutchinson 2007

All rights reserved. No part of this publication may be reproduced, stored in a retrieval system, or transmitted, in any form or by any means, electronic, mechanical, photocopying, recording or otherwise, without the prior permission of the author.

ISBN: 978-0-9556814-0-0

For Bettywho

Published by The Wishing Well

andy@thewishingwell.org.uk
www.thewishingwell.org.uk

Contents

The Wishing Well 7

The Blank Canvas 15

Ohm's Law 21

The Cosmic Priest 29

The Colour of Smoke 41

Semi-Conscientious 49

Equally Insignificant 57

"Will You Marry Me?" 59

Over Egging the Pudding 71

The Missionary Position 81

'B' Shift 89

Preferred Lies 97

The Supergun 103

Underboss and Weeble 109

Joining the Dots 119

When Is A Pint Not A Pint? 125

The Window 131

Chapter 1

The Wishing Well

Billy Hunt was given a key role on the escape committee before the bus had even turned a wheel en route from Linlithgow Academy to Holyrood Palace. As school trips went, this was not expected to be too memorable. Having a fully formed plan on arrival at Holyrood the parties involved made good their escape. Billy led Jackie Morrison, Lanna Green, Eric Forbes and Gordon Sharp toward the prospect of a better day, it happened to lie east. In no time at all they reached a reassuringly scary built-up area of the City of Edinburgh.

They somehow got split up, and Billy ended up on his own on a street of tenements, named East Cross Causeway. The street had a sweet shop, a bar and a baker's outlet. His immediate interest in this street was the sweet shop. He went in, put two Mars Bars, a Crunchie and a packet of chewing gum in his pocket, then took a penny chew to the counter. He waited nervously to be served, held up by a small gap-toothed Betty Boop look-a-like. Once she cleared the stage, he paid for his chew and followed her out of the door. He walked down the street behind her swerving to avoid a collision when she suddenly stopped at the main entrance to one of brighter looking buildings. As he passed by, she pointed to a beautiful stone wishing well and said, "You should make a wish." Girls didn't often speak to Billy so he wasn't about to ignore her although he knew that she would come back out after he had gone and remove his coin from the well. She didn't strike him as being a typical wish seller; she lacked entirely in mystic charm.

He waited until she closed the door behind her, and then dropped 2p in the well. He wished for success and the respect of his peers—not a bad pair of wishes for a 13 year old. On another day he might have wished to be a footballer or to go out with Lanna Green, but being alone in the big city had the effect of making him feel grown up.

Whether it was sod's foresight that made him wish for the two things he would ultimately never have, or whether Betty Boop, as predicted had nicked the coin and in so doing had invalidated his wishes, was irrelevant. What is relevant is that, for reasons unknown, his wishes never came true.

As his friends had gone their own way or ways, he had no idea if they were still together; Billy decided to rejoin the rest of his class at the Palace. School trips bored him, school bored him, everything bored him, he needed to knuckle down and focus on something he could get his teeth into. Anything to distract him from the misery of compulsory education and the torment of being Billy Hunt.

Who would have thought that something as simple as counting would get him through, school, college and all that followed?

The idea of counting came to Billy shortly after he had served out his detention for going missing on the school trip. It turned out his fellow escapees had returned as soon as they had detached themselves from him and had immediately turned Queen's evidence to escape punishment.

He was sitting in a maths class paying scant attention to the teacher who was writing things on the blackboard. A quick glance showed him what he could recognise as being numbers but she put them up in a way that made no sense at all. At primary school he had been quite good at arithmetic, but maths seemed to take liberties with numbers in the way arithmetic never did. Suddenly it became a puzzle and you had to find unknown numbers by manipulating numbers that you did know. Billy felt sure that there would be people who could find the value of x where $2x=6$, and also that even if he figured out how to do it, he would never need to because the people who did that thing would be happy to tell him.

He suddenly became aware that the teacher had stopped at his desk, had sneaked up on him if truth be told, and was looking down at him. "You seem to have drifted off Billy, is there something you are having trouble with here?"

"Well to tell you the truth Miss, I'm not sure I need to know this stuff you are teaching me. Will it have any practical use in my life?"

Miss Lightfoot had heard this question so many times. "Well Billy, what are you going to be if you grow up?"

"I'm not really sure Miss. I hadn't really thought about it. A footballer I suppose."

The boys in the class went into uproar; the girls weren't sure what to do but those looking to impress boys, giggled knowingly. Billy quickly looked to see which girls weren't giggling because they might be considering him as boyfriend material. Oh dear, the glass was definitely half empty. Lanna Green was giggling, that was disappointing.

After restoring discipline in the class, Miss Lightfoot turned her attention to Billy again and gave him a look that he had never seen before but one he would come to recognise later in his life due to the frequency he saw it. He didn't know what to call the look but the closest he could come to equating it to something he knew was the look of Mr Mainwaring in Dad's army when he says, "Stupid boy."

Miss Lightfoot smiled, "Well if you're going to be a footballer you won't need to know any of this Billy. Maybe you should just sit quietly and count all the goals you are going to score for your team."

So he did. He started counting. While it was not known at the time, Billy suffered from a compulsive disorder, so when he started something it had to be obsessively taken to conclusion. He was an all or nothing boy in everything he did. Today Billy is just short of 7,500,000—that works out about 600 a day, which is not fantastic but as an average it is acceptable because some days you just don't get time to count.

There were times even during school days when Billy would not count. He would never count in French or history for example, because the French teacher, Noddy Dunlop, was a psychopath who used to pull pupils' hair and bang their heads against the wall if they upset him, and history was his favourite subject.

Mostly though he would count without a care in the world.

And so, it is important to know that at a very early age Billy Hunt was completely fucked up, and he was fucked up by Miss Lightfoot, who could not be bothered to teach him or even explain to him the importance of being taught.

Although Miss Lightfoot kicked off proceedings, she was too busy to concentrate solely on fucking up Billy Hunt, so she passed the ball to Lanna Green, who took it and ran with it for the next few years.

Disgruntled by all aspects of school life, Billy focused his energies on football and became a regular in the school team, though he was by no means the best player. On Thursday afternoons, the team for the weekend game would be read out by the gym teacher and because Billy played on the left wing, number 11, he always had to wait right until the end to hear if he had been picked. He usually was, but the agony of not knowing until the last moment became a problem to him, and later in life he would always try to avoid getting into situations where the outcome was either in doubt or instant knowledge of the outcome was postponed. Yes, he became a control freak.

And so, by the age of 15 he was a short sighted diabetic control freak with a compulsive disorder, things could only get better.

His least favourite subjects at school were the technical ones, woodwork and metalwork, plus anything relating to science. He possessed the hand skills of a trout with mittens, so on entering 3rd year he wisely opted for French and history rather than physics and applied mechanics. This decision marked both the beginning and the end of his wisdom—unfortunately. For reasons which would never become clear to anyone, he decided at the end of 4th year to apply for a job in engineering, a job which would not fully utilise his extensive knowledge of the Napoleonic wars.

That Billy had already chosen to leave school at the end of 4th year was in itself a contentious issue. He had an elder brother, Anthony, who had done this without any of the concern his own decision invoked, and he had an elder sister, Joan, who had completed 6th year and gone on to university; so the Hunt's had their star.

His father urged that he could do well by furthering his education into 5th year at least, if not 6th year. But his mind was made up even as he started 3rd year, he would leave at the earliest opportunity.

As Billy progressed through the early stages of 3rd year at Linlithgow Academy, he already knew the time and date of his leaving. Apart from constantly reminding his father, he had otherwise kept his counsel for a number of reasons, not least he felt the teachers would try harder and be more focused on his education if they considered him to be Higher Grade or perhaps even university material.

Unfortunately, Billy then let the cat out of the bag during a bizarre exchange with an English teacher named Boris.

Boris was a Hungarian who had learnt English from Shakespeare. He had achieved something of a cult status at the school and was always given the best 30 pupils at the end of 2nd year so that he could educate them to 6th year level. Billy had found himself in the top 30 at selection time, though how he had done this is something of a mystery because he had never read a book of substance in his life. In actual fact, he had never read anything at school at all because he couldn't see well enough to read.

It was Marc Bolan who said, "The man who has never read a book, has no advantage over the man who cannot read." He also said, "Oh, Debra, you look like a Zebra," so his credibility, if not his talent, was questionable.

Billy did have spectacles but chose not to wear them outside the house because he had once been called 'speccy four eyes' and the insult had been very upsetting and hurtful. Based on this one insult Billy decided never to wear glasses in public again, and as this meant he could not read text books at school, his education did suffer to some degree. Once you have not worn glasses for a short time, to then put them on is impossible because to become a speccy four eyes holds far greater stigma than to have always been one.

By the time Billy had reached 3rd year, girls had also become an issue, having a girlfriend was quite important in the measurement of social status. Not wearing glasses would help him for sure, but while decanting spectacles he had failed to act on his bad breath, buck teeth and a hideous haircut, which made finding a girl of suitable beauty unlikely. Then everything changed in what to this day remains Billy's 15 minutes of fame. The verbal exchange which blew up out of nowhere also showed Billy the value of bullshit or 'spin' as it is called today.

Boris, the Hungarian, had set his star pupils the task of reviewing a book they had recently read. Billy chose 'Score and More' a novel about an honest but ageing footballer who had refused to take a bribe, only to find that his son, who played for the same team, had taken a bribe. Despite the potential for moral dilemma, the author John Motson, a football commentator, had chosen to focus more on the footballing aspects, and the book ended with both father and son scoring hat-tricks in the final game of the season, to earn their team promotion. Billy took the path of least resistance and in deference to the fine author he reviewed the football in favour of the underlying issues.

Once Boris had marked the papers he went into performance mode for distribution. He personally handed over the papers of 29 pupils with a comment, all comments were positive, some were congratulatory in tone. He then walked over to the bucket and dropped the last remaining review into it with panache and contempt. "Are all students in possession of reward for their work?" he shouted, forgetting to remain Shakespearean.

"I do not have my paper," mumbled Billy in a quiet low tone.

It is and was even then typical that when Billy's life unravelled it did so in a most glorious way and often his status would rise at the expense of anyone in the way of that rise. "Hunt, you are an ape!" exclaimed Boris. The trigger had been pulled and the bullet was only going to be hitting one person. Self-preservation was and still is Billy's foremost quality. He opened proceedings by stating a fact, never a bad way to build up confidence and credibility while weakening your opponent's argument by having his first comment stricken from the record.

"It may or may not be true to say I am descended from an ape but to say I remain one is incorrect and is beneath you sir."

No one had ever spoken back to Boris and he was rocked by the first exploratory jab. The class also sensed a 'Friends Reunited' moment of biblical proportions, though obviously none knew what 'Friends Reunited' was. They just knew something would be invented one day to do justice to this moment in time.

Boris, still reeling from the shock of a retort, went to pieces and even Shakespeare could not bolt the now open stable door. To say he took up lodging back in the womb would be to overstate, but he did revert to being Hungarian and in trembling voice uttered, "Ficko".

It was only 25 years later when the internet provided a Hungarian to English translator that anyone realised that he had called Billy a dog and not said, "Fuck you!" which was the interpretation adopted in the moment.

Billy rose to his feet, drawing himself up to full height of seven feet six inches (Noddy Holder platform shoes). "You may shout sir, you may use language unsuitable for the classroom and yes you may insult me, but I have only the finest words for you. Through my hard work, (a lie) I have been offered an opportunity coveted by all self-respecting pupils of this academic institution, the opportunity to be taught by possibly the finest English teacher this school has ever known. You sir, teach your pupils at a level beyond ordinary grade, whereas I aim only towards ordinary grade. Therefore we are at odds with our aspirations; but sir, we must not be at odds in our belief that I am entitled to the best education this school can offer, particularly as I have earned that right and undergone the rigours of selection to have the honour of being your pupil. I would have you teach me now sir." The spontaneity of the moment was causing Billy to veer toward Shakespeare and for the one and only time in his life he had the sense to quit while he was ahead.

Boris was shaken; he had been made to look foolish by a scruffy half-blind boy who read large print football books. At the same time he had been paid the greatest of compliments.

In 1941, Horthy and Lazzlo Bardossy had seen appeasement fail and had decided to join Hitler in his ill-advised foray into Russia. Had Boris learned from the folly of his ancestors?

"Hunt, you make your points well and I will be pleased to teach you to the level of your choosing."

The Hungarian had learned and his stock rose accordingly with his pupils. Billy's stock went through the roof.

Before even joining the dinner queue that day he had kissed Lanna Green, the lovely girl who had previously afforded him Israel's right not to exist. Better still, by the time he went to bed that night he was number one on Lanna's list whenever she wanted her hair brushed. She was a strange girl with her hair brushing fetish, but she was not generous with her love, refusing to brush Billy's hair, even though his needed it more than hers. All things considered, she was a looker with nicely forming breasts and Billy was confident that he would touch them one day, when they were complete perhaps.

Despite his successful introduction into the world of bullshit, Billy neither used nor mastered the art to his advantage while at school. The rest of his schooldays were spent in almost total anonymity and he became the weird kid who claimed he had brushed Lanna Green's hair, even though everyone 'knew' Ally Thomson brushed her hair on a regular basis and he asserted the view that he was the first and only one to do so. Ally was fat, wore glasses, had intolerable acne and when aroused could only manage six feet two inches even with his Noddy Holder shoes. If Billy was going to lose hair-brushing rights to a guy like this, he would have to act, and at the end of 4th year his plans to leave school coincided with his belief that earning money would greatly improve his looks where girls were concerned.

And so on May 22nd 1977 at thirteen minutes past two, a date and time of his choosing, he signed the document which freed him of the burden of education. All he needed now was a job, how hard could it be?

Billy applied for three jobs. The first was an apprentice fittership with the Gas Board, based in Edinburgh. The second, an Electricianship with Ferranti, also based in Edinburgh. The third, an unspecified apprenticeship with BP Chemicals in Grangemouth, a factory close enough that he could smell it from his bedroom in Linlithgow.

The Gas Board and Ferranti offered him an interview, while BP offered him an aptitude test at Falkirk College of Technology. He only needed one job so having been given money by his father to attend the interviews in Edinburgh he reallocated these funds to purchases from Revolver Records on Linlithgow High Street. The Gas board got him Tommy—The Soundtrack. He later wished he'd attended the interview instead because it would have been less boring. Ferranti funds got him, Low—David Bowie, and whenever he sees the word Ferranti to this day he still gets a warm glow in recognition of the influence that record still has on his life even today.

Billy put all his eggs in the BP basket. At no time did it occur to him that, having favoured French and history over physics and applied mechanics when making subject choices, he was not ideally suited to an apprenticeship. Surely it would occur to BP though.

Chapter 2

The Blank Canvas

Being one of two-thousand applicants for seventeen BP apprenticeships would save Billy from himself, surely? The first step was the aptitude test at Falkirk College of Technology. Unfortunately this test was not a deal breaker by any stretch of the imagination, for example:

Man 'A' jumps off a diving board 5 feet high. Man 'B' jumps off a diving board 12 feet high. Which man goes deeper into the water? This was one of the more difficult questions so it seemed unlikely that the aptitude test served any purpose other than to weed out those who would turn up from those who would buy records with the bus fare.

Having negotiated 100 questions, Billy left the exam confident he hadn't made a fool of himself, but he couldn't help thinking that many would have scored higher than he had and the engineering door would be firmly closed in his face.

Two weeks passed, and then a letter dropped through the door inviting him to BP Chemicals training centre for an interview. He would learn later that this placed him in the top 50 of those tested. Wow!

In the days leading up to his interview, Billy's father missed no opportunity to remind him this was a big mistake. "You don't even fix your own bike," and "You have no mechanical background, you have no mechanical or electrical subjects in your portfolio." Finally, "You should have stayed on at school."

As motivational speeches go, his father had hit the button. If Bonnie Prince Charlie had delivered such wisdoms before Culloden, the ensuing scuffle may have had a different outcome, perhaps negating his need to dress up as a woman to escape to France—unless he had wanted to of course. No, proving parents wrong is a son's duty and Billy took this duty very seriously. Having said that, he would concede that his father was right in every respect, but that was not the point, what was important, was for Billy to find a way of getting a job he was wholly unsuited to. If he could do it this once, he was confident he would be able to do it at will for the rest of his life. He would rise to the challenge because failure now might set a pattern for life and he was too young with too many years ahead of him to be boxed.

Billy arrived for the first interview of his life in his brother's suit, which fitted him at many cardinal points if not all. He was invited into a small room with a large desk, behind which he saw three serious-looking men. Understanding that the seat at his side of the desk was intended for him, he sat down and then was invited to do so. A bad start and the interrogation had not yet begun. The three characters whose ages seemed proportional to their waste size introduced themselves as Mr Bennett, Mr Jamieson and Mr Marsh. Mr Marsh looked about 60 and ready to pop. The slim Mr Bennett opened by welcoming Billy and telling him not to be nervous and to feel free to ask questions at the end.

Having wondered why someone with his educational background would be invited for interview, his concern was soon put to bed. The tone of the questioning led him to believe that he was a patsy, he was an easy reject, the no brainer, 'he'll never do' candidate.

Marsh, "We don't see anything in your schooling to suggest to us why you are seated here in front of us Billy." Jamieson, "We're going to have to make the aptitude test more difficult,"—this comment aimed at Bennett who seemed hurt and replied, "Maybe you need to actually read the application forms."

Billy took it as a compliment when people suggested that he could, start a fight in an empty room. Without him having uttered a pertinent word, it all kicked off. He watched as the character assassinations developed and was pleased that the focus had gone away from actually talking to him, because questions he did not need right now.

The 25-minute battle drew to a close, and when the protagonists realised he was still there, a severely battered Marsh thanked him for attending, invited him to leave and wished him well.

"Before I go, may I speak, you did say I could ask any questions I might have at the end."

"Of course, I'm sorry please ask away," Marsh beamed in a condescending manner. Remembering not to add, "Then fuck off."

Billy had not anticipated conflict between the men interviewing him, but rather than let it throw him off track, he was able to use it to his advantage. Three men hurting and with damaged egos is not a problem, but a solution opportunity. These guys needed a cuddle.

"Am I right in saying that you three gentlemen are the backbone of the BP training program and that you will guide successful applicants towards their chosen career? That you will do this using programs put in place by your predecessors, programs which with all due respect adopt a paint by numbers challenge."

Jamieson leaned back clasping his hands behind his head and with the air of a tolerant but tiring headmaster said, "Well Billy, that is a very simplistic view, which barely does justice to the system of training which we provide for and on behalf of both BP and the apprentices."

Bennett, "He's got a point though."

Having been told he had a point Billy desperately tried to remember what it was so he could pursue it to conclusion. It came back to him after an uncomfortably long pause. "So let's say, you have a template in place and each year you choose a number of lads who nearly fit the template, then you spend four years chipping the edges off to get a perfect fit. You've made a tradesman out of a prefabricated part. Where's the challenge, what inspires you? When you gentlemen retire," he focused his gaze on the ageing Marsh who now looked 64, "will you not want one story of achievement to tell your grandchildren. I am that story; you will speak of Billy Hunt, the blank canvas that you painted your vision of the future on; the boy with no pre-conceived ideas whom you moulded into one of the finest tradesmen to leave the BP Chemicals training centre. Gentlemen I will leave you with the thought of what you could have done."

As Billy got up and turned to leave, he found his way blocked by Bennett, who had somehow managed to get from one side of the desk to the other in the blink of an eye. "Please sit back down Billy; we still have things to discuss." Jamieson had also risen and had hyperspaced to Hunt's side of the desk, where he now held the chair which Billy was invited to re-occupy.

Jamieson rubbed his chins, "If we were to offer you an apprenticeship right now, would you accept our offer and keep quiet about such a deviance from normal procedure until formal letters have been issued."

Not being one to punish those who underestimated him, Billy was both forgiving and generous in his answer. "You know it's interesting you should say that because, ten minutes ago my answer would have been no, but I have to say you gentlemen have inspired me. I find myself buying into your vision and I have a desire to be a vital spool in the machine you have brought to my mind."

"Don't you mean cog?"

"No I definitely see a machine, with us as the four parts that make it work."

"The job is yours Billy," beamed Marsh with outstretched hand. A wholly undignified amount of back slapping and self-congratulation was in evidence as Billy slipped quietly out of the room.

On the bus home, Billy's joy was tempered with some reality. They had known he was unsuitable, he knew he was unsuitable, so what the fuck was going on here? He decided it was fate and he would go with the flow. Of course he would have to seriously think about the implications of turning up for his first day as a blank canvas. Perhaps he could put a few pre-emptive strokes on the canvas just to help things along in the initial stages. Yes, he would start learning stuff. For example, why both ends of a spanner are exactly the same, what's the point of that, is it in case you break one end, can both ends be used at the same time to speed the job up? It was all very confusing, but it was exciting too. In 4 years' time he would know stuff like this.

The official job-offer arrived in due course and he learned the terms and conditions. A wage of £33 a week, year one; £48 a week, year two; £54 a week, year three; and £59 a week, year four left Billy with little to weigh up, he was going to be an apprentice. Also it seemed that he was to be indentured, which to all intents and purposes meant he could not be sacked, a reassuring clause, which meant he could plan the next four years of his life confidently.

Which trade he would be offered was not yet known. BP was looking for eight instrument mechanics, four electricians, four fitters, and a welder. Billy was required to indicate two preferences in a letter of acceptance, he chose electrician or fitter. The final decision would be made by BP based upon his exam results, these not due to be sent out for another six weeks. He pondered the possibilities. Would he fail enough of his exams to become an electrician, or would he even manage to fail them all and become a fitter? His musing indicated an already healthy contempt for the two trades in question.

Six weeks passed and the exam results dropped through the letter box striking his mother on the back of the head as she bent down to pick them up. He had passed them all, one 'A', four 'B's and two 'C's, being the grades. He wasn't sure where this left him job-wise, would they now reject him? He had heard of people being rejected for things because they were too clever, but this had never happened to him.

BP seemed not to deliberate too long or too hard because a few days later he got a letter telling him, he started on August 15th 1977 as an Instrument Mechanic. He had only two weeks to find out what exactly that was, but he was encouraged when his father told him that it would not be as physically demanding as the other trades which lent themselves to greater physical exertion and dogged stupidity.

August 15th arrived and so did Billy, at ICI, two miles up the road from BP Chemicals.

The person who kindly drove Billy to his correct place of employment introduced himself as John Herd, a pleasant and good-humoured man. It was one of many great ironies in Billy's life that this very man would give him a job at ICI in four years' time when BP threw him out at the earliest moment they could legally do so.

Chapter 3

Ohm's Law

If alarm bells weren't ringing loudly in the BP Training Centre following Billy's late arrival for his first day, then surely they were at the end of his second day. Training officer Bennett asked the apprentices to check in a week before college started, after this week his first year would be spent entirely at college. This induction week would clearly be a getting-to-know-you exercise. A major part of 'getting to know you' would be a small test set on the afternoon of August 16th 1977. In reality then, it was a 'getting to know what you know session', and Billy didn't like the sound of this at all. Why they would employ you and then test you was beyond him. As everyone knows you don't look at car prices just after you've bought one, it can lead to disappointment on a grand scale and for BP it almost certainly did.

As Billy headed for the Training Room where the test was to be held, across the pond, Elvis Presley was just heading to the toilet. One of these diabetics would come out unconscious and the other would come out dead. Would the world lose a great man or would Billy somehow survive his ordeal?

This was no height of diving board test, this was serious stuff. Question 1 asked for an explanation of Ohm's Law. Billy had never come across Mr Ohm in French classes or even history classes for that matter, but the speed of scribbling from his new workmates suggested they were all familiar with the chap. He was immediately presented with a personal multiple choice question, did he:

a) Put his hand up and say, "who the fuck is Ohm by the way?"
b) Say nothing, and leave his test paper blank
c) Lapse into an immediate Diabetic coma.

All things considered, and all options were seriously considered, Billy opted for c) purely on the basis that it never failed, it was feasible and most important it was genuine because the sight of question one had in fact upset his blood–sugar balance. Stress destroys insulin and makes a diabetic go high rather than low, low being the end of the scale which offered him an immediate out. Despite this minor medical detail he was capable of hitting the floor equally well in either state and he hit it with great conviction and with no thought for collateral pain or damage.

If BP had hoped to learn something from this test then it was a success, for this was the first it knew of Billy's diabetes, a medical condition he had completely forgotten to mention at any stage during his recruitment. Being indentured would cover this misunderstanding he felt as he was carried to the medical centre in preparation for onward transportation home.

He was told to take a week off and at this point you would think he might use this time to learn a bit about Ohm and his Law as the two were obviously quite important to BP and for all he knew the rest of industry. But no, the thought never crossed his mind. He was an optimist and he also had a very strange belief that you are never asked the same question twice. Of course he was getting confused with lightening strikes here and on day one at Falkirk College of Technology; Ohm was firmly back on the agenda. More alarmingly it became apparent that for the next four years Ohm was going to keep popping up in many different guises. He seemed to be the key to everything but who the fuck was he and why did industry place such great store in him?

Billy had learned his lesson, now he was going to get to the bottom of it. That would be easier said than done though because you have to remember this was 1977 and you couldn't just Google Ohm. You actually had to know something about the subject to know which library book to steal. He put together the known facts, which were:

a) The Instrument Mechanics were being asked about Ohm
b) The Electricians were being asked about Ohm
c) The Fitters and the Welder were not being asked about Ohm.

He concluded that Mr Ohm had nothing to do with big hammers and gas bottles, he was only important to people with an IQ above 25 and you only needed to know about him if you had at least one 'O' Grade. This was a start, but more research was needed. He would need to learn about Ohm from someone who knew about him, but he would have to ask the question in such a way so as not to let it be known that he knew nothing about him. And so the quest for an answer became the quest for a question and it didn't seem like a problem that could be solved quickly. He needed to buy time; so he stopped all injections of insulin with immediate effect and within two days was safely bedded up at Bangour Hospital, where he could mull the problem over.

After three weeks in Bangour he had finally worked out a solution. He would ask Colin Ross an electrician in the same BP intake, who had by coincidence also been at school with him. He chose Ross for three reasons.

Firstly, he was an electrician so the answer would be given in its most basic form.

Secondly, no one liked Colin Ross so if he told people about him asking the question they would just ignore him.

Thirdly, Colin Ross just needed a friend so badly that he would talk to anyone who showed any signs of liking him.

Billy knew the downside of asking Colin, he would have to listen to Wishbone Ash and discuss aspects of the band's greatness with this lunatic who needed punk rock in his life more than any man alive.

The temptation was to postpone visiting Colin until the last possible moment but this could not be done. He simply could not risk being asked about Ohm's law in the college entrance because in the diabetic world it's three strikes and you're out. Hit the deck again with a blood–sugar balance anything lower than four or higher than nine and he would be thrown out of the British Diabetic Association.

Such a fate would leave him four BDA magazine coupons short of a record token and Bowie was putting the finishing touches to Heroes at the time, pending its release in late-September, which coincided with the collection of the final token. No, the stakes were high, so he decided to go to Ross's house—which was only a mile away—the day before he was to return to classes.

On his way to Colin's house, he met a now fully formed Lanna Green with very untidy hair. Things were looking up and thoughts of Ohm were replaced by thoughts of sorting Lanna's hair problem out. Colin Ross would listen to Wishbone Ash alone this night, as he did every night, Billy had hair to brush.

Short, spotty, fat Ally had left Lanna's hair in a dreadful state and it was two days before a newly sexually educated Billy Hunt saw daylight again.

After all the worry and torment Ohm had caused him, the man seemed inconsequential now that he had realised his penis could do so much more than pee over very high walls. Having given up high wall peeing contests some years ago, it came as a relief to him that he did not have an additional part as useless as his appendix because he figured everything was there for a reason and was losing faith in God, Adam, Eve and Ron Hubbard, whose book he had read as a fallback option in the event of the first three on the list being discredited.

It was interesting how he had come across Ron Hubbard, the founder of the Church of Scientology. In Linlithgow he used to hang around buildings which had been a bomb factory during the war. The buildings were now disused and were perfect for executive gang huts. In Billy's 'apartment', someone, presumably a publisher, had dumped thousands of books, some of which were in new condition, apart from being chewed on by rats. Billy found a book called 'Dianetics' by Ron Hubbard. He assumed the publisher had dumped the book due to a misprinted cover and the book would be about Diabetics, and felt sure it would be a book worth reading having only recently become one. He read the entire book waiting for a connection, which he felt would emerge towards the end, but of course it never did. This was the only 'serious' book that he had ever read and unfortunately it was pish and he read it for all the wrong reasons, reinforcing his view that all books are bad.

The thorny issue of Ohm still had to be dealt with though, because having a girlfriend was one thing, keeping her was another. To keep her meant keeping his job, and indentures, as powerful as they were, lacked the apparent power of Ohm. Another worry was the increasing number of male hairdressers springing up in his home town.

Homosexuality had become legal some years ago, it was now being widely accepted and Billy had no doubt it would soon become compulsory. Was he at risk of losing his girl to a homosexual hairdresser, perhaps not, but what if she happened across an experimentalist or doubter and introduced him to her hair fetish, he could be turned and all would be lost. No, Ohm had to be dealt with once and for all, so he again headed for the Ross homestead in Barton's Hill.

"Hello, Mrs Ross, is Colin in?" As an opening this seemed perfectly friendly and for Mrs Ross to burst into tears and run back down the hallway was an unexpected turn of events. Momentarily Mr Ross appeared at the door and ushered Billy in. "Were you a friend of Colin's?" The past tense suggested that one of them was dead and Billy's immediate reaction was to wish it was himself.

Walking home 20 minutes later with the entire Wishbone Ash collection under his arm, Billy was troubled more than he had ever been troubled before. He was coming to the view that Ohm's Law would haunt him for the rest of his life and he would never know the stock in trade of his new nemesis. Sure, Ross was a twat with no friends but how the fuck was he going to make any by hanging himself, selfish bastard. In the short time he had spent with Mr Ross he had learnt that Colin was finding the college work beyond him and he had become more and more upset until he finally could not face life anymore. It would be true to say that Billy was seriously considering a copycat suicide at this moment but he decided that copying someone like Ross might make him unpopular with the lads, so he was left with no alternative other than to soldier on bravely.

He would later learn that every annual BP intake since 1962 had created one suicide and that the unfortunate event always occurred in the first year, the full-time, theory-at-college year—the meet Mr Ohm year.

It occurred to him that at some point someone should have cast an eye over the syllabus to look for suicide triggers, but this had never happened. If it had happened it was a pretty safe bet that Mr Ohm's sorry ass would have been out of the window long ago.

Could Billy now do that? Could he link the suicides to Ohm? This man, who had made him ill on his first day at work, then put him in hospital for three weeks and was now responsible for the death of a much loved friend and colleague. He decided that the man was too dangerous and had his feet too firmly planted under the table to be messed with.

The safest thing to do was to just ignore him and get through college without knowing anything about Ohm or his stupid law. He would work harder on the other subjects; anyway, he was confident that if Ohm was that important Mr Dunlop, his French teacher, would have mentioned him.

It was time for a new strategy. Learn the system. Review what he knew and learn from that what he needed to know. The answer, it turned out, was in the 'Knowing Nod'.

He had left school at 16 for two reasons, first to earn money and second to get out of the classroom. Objective one was achieved and when he found out that BP Chemicals apprentices were paid more than anyone else, this was a bonus, or so he thought initially. His second reason for leaving school was thwarted in the extreme because he was now sent on one year's block release, four days in workshops and one day in the classroom, though the distinction was not significant because at the end of the day you looked at a teacher all five days. After only a few days it became obvious to all the BP

Chemicals lads that the money was going to cause problems too, as all the other students went out of their way to make life awkward for the 'rich kids'.

For Billy the four days in workshops were tolerable because he didn't have to think too much to connect wires, bash bits of metal and use a lathe, although a little more thought in the latter would have prevented injuries to no less than four apprentices who were hit by flying chuck keys from lathes started by him without them being removed. The one day of theory in a proper classroom was a different matter; Billy hated it with a passion. He decided he would have to understand how the system worked because at first it seemed very strange to him and he couldn't quite get to grips with what he was meant to learn or how he was meant to learn it. Then one Wednesday in an Instrumentation and Control class the penny dropped and a career finally lurched forward from the starting blocks.

The lecturer put up a slide showing a pipe with a strange object inside it called an Orifice Plate. He then started rattling on about some chap called Bernoulli and a principle he had. Basically it seemed that the pressure in a pipe with water flowing through it would be pretty uniform but if you put this orifice plate in and created a restriction the water in the pipe suddenly flowed faster and at the same time the pressure dropped, this all happened just after the restriction. Then further down the pipe things got back to normal. Billy didn't understand this and having decided that he wanted to be good at everything except Ohm's law, which had proved a dangerous subject, he decided to put up his hand.

The lecturer, Mr Farley, seemed astonished and with a trembling voice asked him what he wanted.

"Why?" enquired Billy.

"Why what?" asked Farley.

"Why does the pressure drop as the flow increases?"

The lecturer went pale, then rallied and he uttered words which could have only been learned at teacher training college. "Oh I see we have a comedian."

The class all laughed as if to confirm that the lecturer had indeed identified a comedian. Mr Farley then moved on to the next bit of the book he was reading from but before he could say Venturi, Billy reared again.

"You haven't answered my question sir."

A pause, then, "Look, we are going through basic principles here, stop being disruptive or I will ask you to leave." And at that precise moment the aforementioned penny dropped. The lecturer didn't know, his classmates didn't know, nobody fucking knew. They were all as thick as him. You didn't need to know how stuff worked, just that it did.

Billy quickly flashed back over the past five weeks and suddenly realised something. Nobody had ever asked a question, no valuable knowledge had been offered or even requested and all the guys in his class who were being looked upon as smarter than average were the ones who got the timing of the knowing nod just right.

The nod had to begin just before the lecturer looked at you and reach its zenith on full eye contact then tail off just as his eyes drifted off you. Fuck me, thought Billy, I can do this. The deal is, if you don't ask questions you won't be asked questions, what we have here is a pact of the well paid mutually ignorant. I need a name for this, thought Billy, something to fall back on under pressure, something that will serve well in all situations, planned and unplanned. I will call it bullshit, he decided, and I will become a master of it because this I can learn he confidently predicted.

After learning the system everything fell into place, and his first year at college was a breeze. He nodded with the best of them and even got student of the month in March 1978 for a particularly well-timed nod in Electrical Principles & Theory Level 1, when the lecturer had pulled a rabbit out of the hat by making a 3-phase motor go backwards. They might as well have given him his papers there and then, made him a tradesman and skipped the next three years. Sadly BP didn't see it this way; they still had much torture and torment to offer him, starting in the BP Chemicals Training Centre on August 15th 1978, or year two as they called it.

Author's Notes

Just for the record, Billy Hunt was only ever asked three direct questions in a career spanning nearly 30 years, and all were asked by planners who had no background in engineering and could therefore be excused for their folly.

Ohm's Law states that Voltage is equal to Current * Resistance (V=IR)

You can learn more about Ohm's Law at:
http://www.kpsec.freeuk.com/ohmslaw.htm

If you or someone you know has been affected by not knowing Ohm's law you/they can call The Samaritans on **08457 90 90 90.** Calls are charged at Local Rate and all calls are treated in the strictest confidence. Press option 3 for Ohm's Law Suicide information.

Chapter 4

The Cosmic Priest

The BP Training Centre was on the BP Chemicals site, but eight apprentices from over the fence at BP Refinery were invited to join forces for second-year brutality. Billy knew all these guys from college, but because there were so many apprentices from many different companies he had not actually worked closely with any of them.

All the Refinery lads seemed to have grown more than the Chemicals lads during the summer holidays—and this was to become a problem. As mentioned before, the BP Chemicals lads were now on nearly £50 a week, but shared a training centre exclusively with lads on half that amount. While BP Chemicals managers seemed not to foresee the problem, Billy did, and it was only a matter of hours into day one when it all kicked off. Brian Day, a Chemicals lad, had inadvertently looked at Jock Bennie's (Refinery) screwdriver. As a result all eight Chemicals lads had the shit kicked out of them in the car park at finishing time.

The fight had been seen by training officer Bennett, second in command of training and the next day everyone was called into the meeting room. Having established that looking at someone's screwdriver was not just cause for beating up an entire crew he took decisive action. He banned the Refinery lads from using the BP Chemicals car park for their vehicles. This meant that the Refinery lads would have to park nearly a mile up the road and walk to the training centre. Billy remembered the beating of that night as being one of the most severe.

The whole of second year was spent in fear and it was difficult to focus on learning of any kind other than, how to avoid getting beaten up. What Billy had expected to be a year of fun and comradeship was in fact turning into a nightmare.

His problems were accumulating on all fronts at this time. He had spent so much time observing gay male hairdressers for fear that they might move in of the lovely Lanna, that he was being openly accused of being a 'shirt lifter'. Worse was to follow; it's hard to imagine worse but get this. Lanna had dumped him for a gay female hairdresser and had signed up to exclusive lesbianity. Billy had never considered girls who have a relationship with each other as being gay; it was fairly acceptable behaviour in his eyes. But when not invited to take part or even watch, when rejected as all that is unacceptable in the male species, well, you've let the lads down.

He saw himself as a captain who had been given the responsibility of a new ship, and the ship had gone down, in every way that is just wrong. Comfort can often be gained from the words: 'It's not you it's me.' No such comfort for Billy was forthcoming; Lanna told the world that after sleeping with Billy Hunt she would recommend becoming a lesbian to everyone who had the equipment to carry it off—her way of saying girls he thought.

With constant beatings and rejection he was sinking into a depression that held no prospects of ending soon. Then suddenly it ended. Life was great again, for 5 minutes at least. Billy answered the call of Punk Rock and the three steps to heaven it offers.

1. Listen to and enjoy Punk Rock
2. Give up all aspects of personal hygiene.
3. Form a band.

Billy had only one real friend at the time, Bobby Locke. Bobby worked for ICI and they had become close in their first year at college. They had many things in common not least, everyone hated them.

At Billy's lowest point Bobby told him that he and a friend, Harry Harrison, were forming a band. Harrison was an excellent bassist and Bobby had a set of keyboards. Bobby invited him to take the microphone so a couple of days later Billy went to a music store in Falkirk and took a microphone. The Cosmic Priest was up and running.

Bobby was an unremarkable character in many ways, but in the context of forming a punk band, he was ideal. He could play every note his keyboards were capable of, but seldom in any meaningful order. In the context of being an Electrician at ICI, he was even more unsuited to this than Billy was to his job. Hand Bobby a screwdriver and his first instinct was always to poke himself in the eye with it. His second instinct was to poke the person who handed it to him in the eye. His third and final instinct was to look for a screw, any screw, anywhere, whether it was the right one or not. Everything Bobby came into contact with using a hand tool would fall to bits as he walked away. He seemed to have a penchant for destruction. Despite all of this, Bobby was the most intelligent person Billy had ever met. No one else seemed to notice this; in fact most people treated him as the village idiot's less well schooled brother.

It was Bobby's appearance and manner that hid his undoubted genius. Like Billy, he dressed strangely, had long unruly hair and had a body language problem. The problem being it was a language no one spoke. He appeared lazy, unenthusiastic, and would constantly fall asleep at the sight of a simultaneous equation of any complexity. The difference being that unlike Billy, who fell asleep to protect his pride and dignity, Bobby fell asleep because he was bored, it was beneath his intellect.

It was inevitable that Billy and Bobby would become friends because as individuals they had too many personal shortcomings. As a double act they could light up a room and get everyone's attention.

As a double act they became quite popular and were held in high regard by their peers because while 18 year olds like to talk about doing crazy things, this pair were doers. Nothing, no matter how dangerous or stupid was beyond them. For example, Billy drove his car along Falkirk High Street blasting on his colonel Bogey musical horns after eight pints of lager. But this was not enough, he did it with Bobby Locke sitting on the roof singing 'You'll Never Walk Alone' while drinking from a bottle of special brew. Students of all shapes' sizes and abilities want to do crazy, something to talk about after a board meeting in later life, Billy Hunt and Bobby Locke raised the bar on crazy to a level never seen before.

The Cosmic Priest became the friends' lectern, a focal point from which their chaotic message would be shared. How the name was derived is to this day a mystery, but it was Bobby's name, he chose it. He had originally thought of calling the band Syno, but he was worried that this might be confused with a financial services company which would set up thirty years later, in 2007. The man was a visionary, he had everything covered, well almost everything. His vision was so focused he allowed one small 'here and now' detail to slip his mind. This was the fact that The Cosmic Priest was the worst band ever to form, and in the punk era that was some achievement. Billy was the singer, but he could not sing and was always too drunk to remember what he was meant to sing. Bobby on keyboards managed to produce the most awful screeching sound ever to come from a musical instrument. Finally there was Harry Harrison on bass guitar. Harry could play, he could play well, but the only interest in his life at that time was fiddling with the contents of his underpants. He would even play one handed to free up his right hand for that purpose.

An article about the Cosmic Priest appeared on the internet some years later, it read:

'October 2nd 1978 remains in the memory of no one save for these three young hopefuls of the Linlithgow and district music scene. On this day at 8pm The Cosmic Priest performed for the first, last and only time at St. Michael's Hotel.

The doors opened at 7:45pm and closed again at 7:46pm as stewarding issues, promotional lapses and a light drizzle ensured few people would see this band perform four songs, none of which any of them knew.

Billy Hunt had written all but three of the four songs they would perform that night but he had unfortunately not bothered to learn the words to any of them.

The first note—though it was not recognised as being a musical note at the time—was struck at 8pm on the dot. The final note being struck five minutes later. It could be said that The Cosmic Priest did not enjoy commercial or any kind of success due to limitations in their line up, in fact they didn't have a drummer or guitarist. It could also be said that they were too far ahead of their time, but it is in fact only said that they were just shite.

Their five minutes of 'fame' behind them, Hunt went back to his miserable existence in the BP training centre, Locke went back to a similarly miserable existence at ICI, and Harry Harrison went back to bed, where he remains to this day.'

This article has been widely accepted as the best thing ever to come from the band's brief existence.

The only other written record of the band is an accidental interview Billy gave to a local fanzine. The publication had done no research but liked the name and assumed with such a good name, this band would be worth talking to.

As well as the interview the fanzine also published the lyrics to 'I Am a Looney', a song written by Hunt and Harrison. It went:

I am a looney, I am quite insane,
I'd rather like to squeeze your brain,
I am a looney, I am a looney

Too many people forcing me around,
Trying to find out where I was found,
Too many people trying to make me work,
What do you think I am, a fucking jerk

I am a looney, I am a looney

They all got their morals wrong,
They must be one hell of a strong,
Can you tell me in which direction,
My mind is going round the bend

I am a looney, I am a looney

When asked to explain the meaning of the song and the message it conveyed, Billy realised that his lyrics were too deep for the punk scene and did not feel disposed to answer either question. For reasons unknown he felt compelled to say instead, "Do you really want me to break both your fucking legs with a baseball bat."

Billy instantly became the guy no one wanted to interview and immediately returned to anonymity and obscurity.

A shit job, no girlfriend, and his dreams of stardom shattered, Billy decided to reappraise his life and move it in a new direction. He had no option other than to continue with his apprenticeship but he needed something good to balance all the bad stuff in his life. Quite by accident he discovered that alcohol gave meaning to life and before the bells brought in 1979 he was an alcoholic attending weekly meetings where he was able to make new friends who shared common interests.

Whatever life threw at him, he always seemed to land on his head.

The second year of his apprenticeship just became a blur. If asked about it today, he could put his hand on his heart and say, "I don't remember a thing."

This was not strictly true because Billy did remember the 'shithouse poet' and during second year the man became an inspiration to him.

Every factory has a frustrated wordsmith who will share what he believes to be his true calling on the toilet walls.

A shithouse poet sometimes sticks to one cubicle, it represents his book of poems, but John James Hamilton was different and his work appeared site wide.

He was born in 1931. No one could have foreseen that a child born in the Grangemouth ghettos would become arguably the finest poet BP Chemicals would ever employ.

While his career with BP began in 1948, his first known poem did not appear until late 1976. It was in November of that year when, 'The Coo', thought to have been written two years earlier first appeared in trap four of the gents in the Phenol Plant. The Coo was a complex poem which many feel gave an insight into John's own character. The lasting legacy of the poem is that long after it had faded from the toilet wall, many who saw it can recite it from memory in word perfect fashion. It had a simplistic Yellow Submarine quality making it a once-read-never-forgotten work.

It read:

Upon a hill, I see a coo
It must have moved
For it is no there noo

His style was unconventional, three line poems being rare and none of the more established poets whose work has been published for mainstream consumption would ever take such risks.

It would be three years before John's work would be seen again, this time in trap two of The Benzene plant toilet. By the time of his second poem, John was a broken man. He declared he had 'lost confidence', having been caught signing off job completion certificates while on holiday in Spain. It was a cruel quirk of fate that BP protocol dictated that anyone signing off work had to physically be at the site where the work had allegedly been carried out. It was perhaps due to this, though many attributed it to burnout, that 'I am a poet' received such poor critical acclaim, being described as self-gratifying, over commercial and shallow by one welder.

John never wrote again after the failure of the poem which has become more widely known as the Benzene work.

There were rumours of a third poem, but this was never found, and in all probability it does not exist. The mention of it though is enough to keep this great man's memory alive.

By the end of second year, Billy had tired of waiting for more poems to appear and though imitators would leave shabby unpalatable work on toilet walls around the site, they were intentionally or unintentionally dishonouring the man. At least Billy had one worthwhile memory of a horrible year in his life.

Third and fourth years were a mix of four days' work experience on the various BP Chemicals plants and the dreaded day release at Falkirk College.

These years would shape Billy's immediate if not long-term future and it all went horribly wrong from the outset. He was still drinking heavily and the extra money being a third-year apprentice provided would enable him to extend his drinking hours. He already had evenings covered so he had to use daytime hours. On work days this meant just an hour at lunchtime, but he managed well enough.

By the end of fourth year Billy, had scraped through his exams, broken more plant than any apprentice in history—with the exception of Bobby Locke along the road at ICI—and he had fallen out with every person he came into regular contact with. Then, things got a whole lot worse. To his amazement, he was told he would not be kept on by BP and that his job prospects appeared pretty bleak.

Adversity had always brought out the best in him and after an initial phase of understandable despondency he rallied once more to the call of a seemingly impossible challenge. He had beaten Boris, he had beaten the three not-so-wise-men to get into BP, and he would beat whoever they chose to give him his leaving papers.

He was asked to attend a meeting in the office of Robert McGregor, an Electrical Engineer, on July 5th 1981 to be told of his dismissal officially. Having been told he could have a shop steward in attendance he arranged a meeting with his full-time official on the 4th to discuss tactics.

The shop steward was quite negative at the meeting and offered little by way of advice or optimism. This did not matter to Billy because he had already formulated his plan and preferred to present himself alone. A shop steward's presence he felt would lend to an atmosphere of confrontation and his plan was best suited to an amicable environment. He would be firm but forgiving because McGregor was only the messenger and when he had finished the messenger would relay to BP their folly and all would be well.

On the morning of the 5th, he walked confidently into McGregor's office and immediately put his foe on the back foot by offering a handshake followed by a remarkably sober and sincere "Good morning Robert." He was ahead on points before he even sat down. There followed a few minutes of general chat before the meeting moved to discussions of the matter at hand.

"Billy, I have the sad task of conveying to you that BP Chemicals has decided not to offer you employment on completion of your apprenticeship. You will of course receive indentures and good wishes from the company and you will be free to explore other opportunities. The company will give you time off to attend interviews and should you find employment before your finishing date the company will consider any request for early release up to a maximum of one month before your official leaving date of 14th August 1981, which is in fact only about 5 weeks away."

He continued, "For my part, I would like to say a few words and express some personal thoughts which I hope you will accept in good grace.

"I first met you in 1979, just two years ago, when you were given an onsite role within the factory and it was decided that you would complete your training in areas of the plant under my control. In the two years I have known you I have found you to be a complete waster, an unreliable lunatic, and a disrespectful and scruffy young man who has made me question my faith in humankind. I would just like to add that I personally can't wait to see the back of you. While you are entitled to say a few words at this point I'd much prefer that you just fuck off out of my sight and with any luck I will never see you again."

Billy felt the need to correct McGregor on a few points before launching his rescue plan. "Well Robert before I have my say let me respond to your specific comments. I was a waster long before you met me so don't sit there like you're the man who discovered this and brought it to the world's attention. You say I am an unreliable lunatic, can I ask if you have ever met a reliable lunatic, because I suspect you have not. You therefore imply that I'm some sort of weird and different lunatic, which simply isn't true. Finally you suggest I am scruffy but are you familiar with the saying, never judge a book by its cover. I once found a book entitled Dianetics, I thought it was about Diabetics but it turned out, 625 pages later not to be the case—so you see what I mean."

"No I don't actually because the cover was right."

"Yes, a bad example. Anyway to move on, I'd like to inform you of some facts relating to my current situation. I am a diabetic and BP states that it has a policy of employing disabled or partly-abled people at a level of 2% of the total workforce. It therefore makes sense that I contribute to that 2% since I am better than people with no arms or legs, or who dribble and need to be helped to the toilet. A man who can help meet the quotas and wipe his own arse is a valuable commodity for a company pretending to be compassionate. Secondly, I am an alcoholic and BP therefore has a duty of care owing to me. I am currently in a treatment programme so I can't be sacked for not having met the company's policy on this matter."

"You've never actually informed the company that you have a drink problem to my knowledge," clutched McGregor at a passing straw.

"Jesus Christ man, I've been turning up at work pissed for nearly 2 years now, don't you think you should have noticed? I can't do your job for you; I have enough on my plate."

"We just thought there was something wrong with you, that you were a bit simple maybe."

Billy had promised himself he would remain calm but this was too much. "A bit fucking simple? I was drunk; I didn't even know I was here most weeks until I saw my pay packet. I'm sorry Robert but this reflects very badly on you as my boss. I think you ought to consider how the company may view your role in all of this. That we find ourselves in this situation today is as much your doing as mine."

McGregor went pale; the man knew he was beaten. "These are personnel issues and I can't comment on them but I will relay your statements to our human resource people and get back to you with their views on the matter."

Billy left the office full of confidence but he was not a fool and he knew the best thing to do with an advantage was to press it home.

The final element of his failsafe rescue plan was flawless and so well planned it could not possibly go wrong. He would start a small fire on the Ethanol plant, then discover it, put it out at great personal risk and be a hero. The papers would run stories for weeks on the hero who had saved Grangemouth. It would be impossible for BP to get rid of this selfless, brave young man without incurring the wrath of the nation.

He saw the Daily Record headline. "Multinational giant to sack young hero who saved Grangemouth."

Yeh, right, that wasn't going to happen.

Having worked on the Ethanol plant during his 4th year, he had taken quite a liking to the stuff. He knew exactly what proportions to mix the product with lime but he had never actually seen it burn because setting fire to the stuff was in breach of Health and Safety regulations. To say putting a match to it was an eye opener would be the understatement of all time. The Americans spent billions on an atom bomb; all they needed was a match and a bucket of Ethanol. The Grangemouth sky glowed orange for three weeks.

Before the flames were even doused fingers were starting to point in Billy's direction. The enquiry that followed the fire commented on his singed eyebrows, but it failed to mention that everyone within a 12-mile radius of Grangemouth also had singed eyebrows.

He was eventually cleared of any wrongdoing when he was able to convince a hearing that he was and always had been incompetent, and more than that, was able to support this claim with documentation and written testaments. Despite having his good name intact, the horror of the tragedy haunts him to this day, particularly as two brave young firemen had committed suicide by inhaling smoke on the first night of the blaze. He felt guilty in some ways but in his heart he knew he was just another victim of the Ethanol tragedy.

BP stuck to their guns and on 31st July 1981 he was unceremoniously released. The company finally agreed to give him a reference which he would be able to take to prospective employers in future. It read:

'Billy joined BP as an apprentice Instrument Mechanic in August 1977. During his time with BP the company had no difficulty providing boiler suits which fitted him as he is of a regular size. Billy has a car and he wears contact lenses to correct short sightedness in his left eye. His family own a lovely dog called Honey, a beagle I think.

I would urge anyone considering offering employment to Billy to contact me personally as I would be happy to answer any questions and provide more information than can be written here.'

The reference was signed by Robert McGregor no less, and Billy felt he may have misjudged the man. Offering to speak to any future employer was very decent of him and he had not written anything bad, which Billy was afraid he might.

To be one of the chosen few from thousands of applicants for a BP apprenticeship and then to throw it all away was criminal, but Billy was pragmatic enough to realise that the fault lay entirely with BP—who should not have chosen him in the first place. At least it would learn from this he felt, and would not make the same mistake again.

Incredibly, within 4 years Billy Hunt was back in BP boiler suit working for the company at one of the world's largest oil terminals.

The four years preceding his reconciliation with BP pathed the way for both parties to have a better relationship, and to grow their mutual, if sometimes taught respect for each other.

His next move was to go to the gatehouse where he had appeared four years earlier in error. The gatehouse of ICI, and this time he would be going in.

Chapter 5

The Colour of Smoke

Why ICI, the second largest employer in Grangemouth would recruit Billy Hunt who had just been rejected by the largest was never clear. Either they saw something in him, unlikely, or they were just desperate, probable. Anyway, it was on August 25th 1981 that Billy turned up at the same gatehouse he had turned up at in error four years earlier. Destiny then, must also be considered.

Following a brief induction, he was assigned to the East Side maintenance supervisor, a good man who was in charge of S Shed, D Shed, B Shed, G Shed and a maintenance workshop. His empire was a sadly dilapidated collection of barely productive units, none of which had seen a new instrument since the early 1950s.

ICI also had a West Side, these sides being separated by a main road. The West Side was more modern and it was the place to be, but Billy was just happy to have a job and decided he would keep his powder dry, prove himself and then find a lollipop man to take him across the road.

The great thing about working for ICI was that his best mate Bobby Locke worked there and Billy envisaged good times for the two pals working and playing together. Unfortunately Locke was released by ICI in much the same way as Billy had met his fate at BP, and he decided to go to University for the next 20 years. In actual fact, after 20 years of study the University was so sick of teaching him they decided to employ him and Bobby Locke is now a Professor at Napier University in Edinburgh.

Billy spent his first days at ICI in the workshop, where he was clearly being weighed up. He was then assigned to S Shed, the least modern unit in the museum, and given a week to read some manuals, speak to some operators, and generally get to know his area.

It became obvious to Billy from his research that S Shed produced three main things, white smoke and black smoke, which were exported to the Grangemouth sky, and green dye, a seldom seen product which was exported to Japan for army uniforms. The production of green dye apparently coincided with white smoke production, so Billy deduced that black smoke should be kept to a minimum as it seemed not to serve any useful purpose.

Clearly the key to success was to find the device that changed the colour of the smoke and he soon found it. It was a big noisy machine which had a four-foot cam, with an outer cam follower plate which could be adjusted by means of changing the tension on the many springs which sat between the two plates. Billy was optimistic, adjust springs, make white smoke, and produce small amounts of green dye. What could be simpler?

Well, as it turned out, devising a method of getting men to Mars and back in a Reliant Robin could be simpler. He soon found that any single spring adjustment would have an effect on all the other springs and that you really had to just move them all a wee bit, then go outside, look up and hope for white smoke. To Billy, white smoke became an enigma, a rarely seen enigma, but there were successes. In February 1982 there was a prolonged period of white smoke lasting for 3 weeks, which coincided with the production of 2.6kg of green dye, enough to put thirty two Japanese soldiers to muster. On hearing this news, Billy returned from his holidays full of renewed optimism, but a few days later, the black smoke returned and he once again became despondent.

Apart from the challenge of creating white smoke, ICI had little to enthuse him and he became bored and unsettled in a very short time. The introduction of a chip machine was a brief hiatus from the drudgery of life in a dirty and noisy factory built during the Second World War.

There were few young people in the workforce as anyone with ambition moved on very quickly. It felt like he was in God's waiting room 60 years before his appointment time.

Things did liven up for a few short weeks in the Spring of 1982 when Sir Clive Sinclair, a bampot of the first water, released his ZX81 personal computer. It was available as a ready-assembled, switch-on-and-become-confused item, or a build-it-yourself kit item. Confusion occurred earlier in the latter because Sinclair decided to keep some bits back for a laugh. Billy and his boss both bought the kit and set about assembling them during their lunch break. It was the first time his boss had ever seen him wield a soldering iron and their lunch time projects had to be abandoned as the casualty list grew.

As it happened, this had been a lucky escape for Billy. There was a small part of his brain that loitered around doing nothing harmful and was best left dormant. This little piece of incorrectly wired tissue was waiting to be activated by contact with computers. Had it actually recognised the ZX81 as being a computer it would have woken up right there and then, and Billy's life would have been ruined much sooner.

The Chart Changers, who had caused computer building activities to be stopped, were men employed solely to replace circular charts on recorders every 24 hours. They were very old and were unable to move from their chairs once seated and as a consequence could not evade the flying molten solder that constantly flicked off Billy's iron. If BP had a compassionate policy of employing 2% disabled and partly-abled, then ICI put them to shame. At ICI 90% of the workforce were spastics.

In frustration Billy requested a move to the more modern West Side where people talked of electrical instruments and hot showers. His application was rejected though, when it was pointed out that people had been on the list for 20 years and he had only been at the factory for a few months. It was however indicated by nod and wink that white smoke would not do his chances any harm if he were to ask again when his hair was greyer. This seemed to be at odds with sound management thinking which he had always understood to follow the lines: find out what someone is good at and keep them doing it. Why would an ability to produce white smoke and consequent green dye get him out of S Shed, it didn't make any sense.

Having said that, what could he do, personal pride dictated that he would want to create white smoke so that he was not a failure. He persisted with his attempts to tame the springs and the cam follower. He would never give up he decided until either he or the machine broke.

Breaking point, literally, came on May 16th 1982. He was carefully adjusting Bert, he had by this time given names to all the springs, when suddenly the spring broke, sending two pieces through the west wall of S Shed towards Falkirk. He threw his tools down in dismay and walked out of S Shed towards the human resources office where he would resign. Turning around for one last look at S Shed he saw the most amazing thing, pure white smoke. He had dreamt of this moment and he knew exactly what to do, he ran to the workshop and grabbed a welder, who he'd placed on standby many months earlier. They collected up a box of pre-prepared steel plates and ran to S Shed. Billy stood at the doorway looking skywards as the welder tacked the plates onto the springs to prevent them from ever moving again. The welder called, one—Billy called white; the welder called two—Billy called white; and so they went on; forty-two, white; forty-three, white; forty-four, white. Finally the welder attached the final plate, sixty-four, he shouted—black, replied Billy.

As strange as it sounds, he felt a surge of relief, finally it was all over, the outer cam was now stuck in position forever and there would never be white smoke again. Hope and possibility were removed and his suffering was at an end. He walked out of S Shed, retracing his steps to the human resources office where he offered his resignation. ICI thought long and hard before declining to accept his offer of resignation in favour of sacking him. They had been very keen to get words like incompetent, liability and gross misconduct onto the final documents and his resignation would not have enabled them to do so.

Billy handed in his gate-pass at the cash office and was amazed when asked, "What would you like to do with your pension?"

"What are the options?" he asked.

He was told he could freeze it and then when he was 65 he could draw what would amount to about 17p per week relative to 1982 money. Alternatively he could cash it in there and then. In doing so he would receive £57.62. Mental note, arithmetic worth learning, maths, waste of time. "I'll take the money now please."

Having lost jobs with the number one and the number two companies in Grangemouth he felt he needed to review his life choices and perhaps even recalibrate them.

Option 1—continue trying to be an Instrument Mechanic, keep a trade, and stick with something he knew, something he had proved himself at. The first two arguments were sound but the latter two needed some thought. Something he knew? Clearly this was not the case. Something he'd proved himself at? Yes, proved himself to be useless at.

Option 2—turn his back on Instrumentation and do something else. But what?

At this point in time, a couple of people were making news, the aforementioned lunatic, Clive Sinclair and an entrepreneur named

Alan Sugar. Both had started with nothing and were on the brink of vast fortunes, not to say knighthoods. He also had nothing, so clearly he was ideally suited to follow in these men's footsteps. Clive was inventing stuff so he was immediately ruled out as a role model. As far as Billy was concerned, by 1982, if it hadn't been invented it clearly wasn't needed. No, he thought, the world had all the stuff it needed, what about Sugar? He was a far more interesting proposition because he was simply buying and selling stuff.

He studied the Sugar model for days and left no stone unturned in getting at the secret to his success. As it turned out, it was incredibly simple. Buy something for £1, and then sell it for £2. Repeat the process 50 times a week and the money would soon catch up with his counting—and already he was nearing 2 million.

In the book 'Sweet Taste of Success' by Alan Sugar, the author/entrepreneur told of how he worked hard in menial jobs while he grew his empire. Step one, thought Billy, would be to get a menial job or two. He soon secured three evening shifts a week at The Star & Garter Hotel as a barman, and a Saturday job at Revolver Records, the small shop he frequented in his home town of Linlithgow.

As it turned out, although he had not put much thought into the jobs, they turned out to be ideal for his purposes. He was able to drink all he could hold at the Star & Garter—and often more than he could hold—so this saved money as well as paying money. The record shop would help him in his empire building because it was directly related to the product he chose to buy and sell. His business plan was simple and foolproof.

He bought boxes of 100 random albums from an address he'd found in a magazine. Each box was just £5, just 5p per record. These albums clearly stated that they were mixed, there may be more than one copy of a particular album and not all the records were new.

Obviously record companies, record shops and people were dumping their crap on a reseller who simply boxed what he received and sent out lucky dips to entrepreneurs like Billy.

The second stage of his plan was to buy a licence for a pitch at Ingliston Sunday Market, where he would sell the albums as single entities, not as job lots which would have impacted on revenue.

At this time he lived in a small one-bedroomed flat on Linlithgow High Street, so he set about converting his home into a property fit for a young entrepreneur. He moved his bed into the living room and turned the bedroom into an office. Having completed the conversion he stood at his desk, which he had purchased through the 'Under a tenner' column in the local paper and waited for Sunday to arrive, his first day of trading. If all went well he might be sitting at his desk by Monday.

On his first Sunday, he paid £15 for a pitch adjacent to the Edinburgh airport main runway and set up his stall. By close of trading he had sold 20 records at an average price of 50p.

To only lose £5 on his first day was encouraging and he could not wait for next Sunday to arrive. He had always felt that his first two weeks would be an exercise in familiarising himself with his client base. He wondered about creating a customer database and sending out mail shots, but the Ingliston market shoppers proved reluctant to give personal information and bank details when buying a record for 50p.

After just three weeks, he knew the market, it was a nonexistent one. He needed better records. Where could he get better records? At Revolver of course but he had one problem with this, he was not a thief, well actually he was but nevertheless he was reluctant to steal from his new employer. Then it hit him, a plan that would give him saleable stock and would not involve a sudden and dramatic reduction in Revolver stock. He would simply swap his copies of Stylophone Hits by Rolf Harris with Revolver's copies of Johnny the Fox by Thin Lizzy. It was not stealing, it was just stock rotation and the owner of Revolver had told him on his first day, "The only way my shop can survive is if we keep the stock turning over." Turning over? For the next 3 months it was positively spinning.

As sales fell at Revolver, Billy was cleaning up at Ingliston. A remarkable thing really, because he was just learning about business and the shop's owner had been doing this for years. It occurred to him that maybe he was just very good at this and that he had found his calling, he really was an entrepreneur. He was going places.

The first place he was going was Saughton Prison, and he arrived on January 15th, 1983, to take up employment for Her Majesty in the library, a position which came with residential status. The job was one of the better ones on offer at Saughton, though the pay was poor. He'd been told he would be employed in the library for 2 months, but as it happened he was released after just 28 days. It was all very confusing, BP and ICI had let him go for being bad and Saughton let him go for being good. He just could not seem to hold down a job whatever way he played it.

His release happened so suddenly that he never got a chance to say goodbye to Razor McGurk or Big Bubba, who had kindly helped him stop smoking by taking his tobacco from him. It was that kind of community in many ways, caring.

Things had changed while he was away. Margaret Thatcher was growing in confidence having won a war and she decided that too many British people were working hard when they could be taking things a bit easier. Billy joined 3 million others who had been given the chance to relax a bit more. He didn't want to relax seven days a week though; so he returned to his stall at Ingliston each Sunday and ironically he now enjoyed greater success due to a new market economy that was emerging, one where nobody could afford to buy good stuff anymore and had to turn to more modestly priced copies of good stuff.

At the peak of his market trading powers in the winter of 1983 he suddenly and inexplicably made another life changing decision, he would give industry one last chance to benefit from his skills. If it chose not to take it this time he would have nothing more to do with it. He applied for a job with a contractor in Falkirk called Craig Services. Compared to BP and ICI they might be small, but he was confident that if he applied his magic they would not be a small company in a few years. They weren't.

Chapter 6

Semi-Conscientious

As a BP and ICI employee Billy had often peered down his nose at the contractors from Craig Services a small Falkirk-based firm which did the less palatable jobs on these sites. Though in the past he had felt superior with his multinational-badged, laundry-washed boiler suit, it never occurred to him when he applied for a job with the firm three years later that he may be in regression.

A week after posting what amounted to a begging letter, he found himself being interviewed by a victim of his past life sneering, and this guy remembered. The 'interview' lasted 2 hours and it was only the fact that he had no pride that he was able to cope with the early more abusive stages of the ordeal. It might also be said that he thought he was interviewing well because his arrogance and self-belief, though misplaced were total in their conviction.

He was cross-examined by two of the company's directors and this pleased him because he had never even met the directors of BP or ICI. Norman Simpson was a quiet and vindictive man who took pleasure in whispering his questions at a level impossible to detect with the human ear—which was all Billy had. George Shaw was a much more outgoing fellow who was less vindictive than his colleague but much more cynical.

As a double act, these guys were sensational, they could have taken their show on the road. The first part of the interview was purely technical which made no sense to Billy because he knew Craig Services were only called upon to do menial shitty jobs that company staff would not entertain. He could run cable tray and dig holes, what more did they want. He played their game anyway and gave the best answers he could.

It was the second part of the interview where he was able to make an impression. It was his decision to be honest regardless of the consequences which turned the event in his favour.

Shaw kicked off the important questions. "How many RoSPA Gold Awards did you win at BP?"

"Two"

"How do you feel about the safety culture at BP and ICI?"

"I treat it with the contempt it deserves. They are not children's playgrounds, they are industrial sites, if you lose a couple of fingers for the cause, so be it, grow them back and get on with the job I say."

Both men immediately perked up and softened visibly in their demeanour towards him.

Simpson became audible in his excitement, "You see a welding plant on the tank farm at BP, it has been there for two days and no one is using it, do you report to BP that they are wasting money on plant hire when the equipment is lying idle?"

"No, I hook it up to the back of the van and get it out of there. I bring it to your workshop, I work late painting it a different colour, I remove the serial number and any other identifying markings, then I stick an Craig Services badge on it before going home with the satisfaction of a job well done."

It is not entirely clear whether Simpson pissed himself at this point but Billy was pretty sure he had. He was told that he was the first person in Craig's history to win employee of the month at an interview. He was given coffee and biscuits and told to report for work on Monday morning. The only surprise was that he was told to turn up with his own safety clothing and hand tools. This was a different world to the one he had known.

Undeterred he went out and bought a flame retardant tee-shirt and a small screwdriver.

His first job with Craig Services was mounting cable tray from the top of a 300-foot flare stack to ground level. It was December and he really could not decide for a while whether the tee-shirt or the screw driver had been the biggest mistake.

It would be fair to say that Billy was a complete idiot but it would also be fair to say that not many employers would send a diabetic up a 300-foot flare stack with only a tee-shirt, a screwdriver and a cheese roll, telling him it wasn't worth climbing all the way down for lunch then back up, so he may as well eat up there. Within 5 minutes of arriving up in the clouds on the first morning, a welder shot blasted his cheese roll into oblivion.

Billy was being paid 8p an hour extra for height money but he later found out that if he had fallen the height money would be recalculated as he dropped and would stop completely at the precise moment he hit the ground. Craig Services provided a much needed reality check for him and it did him the world of good. For a while he began acting responsibly and even became semi-conscientious.

Despite its understandable initial dislike of Billy, over a period of time Craigs warmed to him and not just because of his attitude to safety and liberation of other companies' property—no, more than this, he was crawler who would sell his granny for the cause.

Having realised he was stupid enough to do anything they wanted, he was offered the Water Board contracts. These were two maintenance agreements with Fife and Central water boards to service their Kent Commander flow recorders. Both water boards hid their instruments all over their respective counties usually in valleys under manhole covers.

Without wishing to get technical there's something you need to know about the Kent Commander Circular Chart Recorder and how it works.

The Kent Commander measures and records flow by detecting a high pressure on one side (connected upstream of an inline pipeline restriction) and a lower pressure on the other side (connected downstream of the pipeline restriction). The greater the flow in the main pipeline the greater the difference in pressure.

So, as the flow gets greater the pressure difference measured is greater and the further up the chart the pen is driven. To calibrate for zero on this instrument there is a really handy thing called an equalising valve. If you close off one of the pipes from the HP or LP side of the restriction and open the equalising valve, the pressure difference is zero; so you can set the pen on the zero line of the chart. It's really clever stuff and it seemed doubtful to Billy if anyone would ever come up with anything better. But there was a slight flaw. For some reason the water wasn't allowed to come into direct contact with the thing that measured the high pressure and low pressure (diaphragm); so what they did was they put mercury in as a buffer. This was not a problem unless you opened the equalising valve before shutting off one of the pipeline valves. If you did happen to get this wrong the high pressure water rattled in pushing the mercury through the equalising valve and out though the low pressure isolation valve and into the pipeline. That's not a good explanation really but it is background to what happened next in the life of Billy Hunt. For six months he introduced to both Fife and Central Region water supplies a healthy dose of mercury, or more accurately, an unhealthy dose of mercury.

We will never know if many or any people died as a result of mercury in the drinking water system, making Billy Hunt the Harold Shipman of Instrumentation. All we do know is that the instrument was not idiot proof and if anyone was going to discover that then he was the man.

It was during a spot check by the Fife Water Board's safety officer that the problem came to light. Meetings were held in the aftermath and the Water board had discussions with Craigs on how best to handle the situation. Billy was invited to the final meeting where he was told that both parties had decided that it was not in the public interest to tell people they had been poisoned and they would just sack him and leave it at that.

Billy agreed with their way forward but felt that another option could be considered. His proposal was that he be sent to work at Mossmorran where Shell and Esso had major, high paying construction works ongoing and where Craig Services had been invited to supply as many warm bodies as they could muster. Such an eventuality would take his mind off the catastrophe he had caused and would make him less likely to feel guilty and run to the papers to confess all. Both Craigs and the water board saw wisdom in his proposal and within a week he was earning £10 an hour instead of £4 and his memory of Kent Commanders was distant and fading.

Having never bought a car costing more than £250, Billy decided that working at Mossmorran not only entitled him to spend decent money on a car but as the plant was 40 miles from his home he would actually need a decent car. He didn't need to worry about wandering round garages either, because he knew exactly what he was going to buy, a Triumph TR7. A couple of years earlier he had been given some brochures on the TR7 and he just fell in love with it. It was best to ignore the reviews in the car magazines which to a publication pointed out its many faults; not least that it was death trap on wheels. It just looked great and the interior was incredible, if it wasn't so small you could happily live in this car.

Against his better judgement he decided to involve his motor mechanic brother Anthony in the deal. He asked Anthony to pick out the best three TR7s for sale in Scotland or even Northern England at a push, and then make appointments for them to go along and view the cars. He would kick the tyres a bit while Anthony checked for other potential problems.

Two weeks passed before Anthony presented himself at Billy's door saying, "Get your cash we are going to get a dream car."

Anthony drove them to Bathgate and they soon found the seller's house. The first thing Billy noticed was a weird looking car on the drive, one like he'd never seen before. He squeezed past the monstrosity and headed towards the garage pleased to assume the TR7 slept indoors at night.

"Whoa, wait, where are you going Billy?" shouted Anthony, "this is the car I wanted you to see."

"What the fuck is that, for a TR7 it isn't."

"This bro' is a Dutton Pheaton. It is a kit car."

Billy could not hide his despair because every time he involved his 'expert' brother in a car purchase he ended up with a crock of shit. "It has no roof, no doors, a wooden floor—"

"I know its awesome isn't it," enthused Anthony.

Billy was beaten and he knew it. "Fuck it, what's the point, there, give the man his money and let's get it home." He handed over £1400 cash and starting figuring out how to get into his new car. With no doors you'd think that wouldn't be a problem but you had to kind of climb in at an angle then slide down into the cockpit. He was not concerned in the least that getting out if an accident occurred might present a problem. He realised that if the car so much as hit a fox it would simply disintegrate around him leaving him sitting in the middle of the road.

Driving back home Billy's first impression was that the back of the car was in a hurry because it kept trying to overtake him. If you so much as touched the throttle the car would just spin around. His brother explained that this was because it had a 1600GT Cortina MK II engine in but it only weighed 22 stone 12 pounds, and that was with them in it. He also explained that it would be best not to take it out in the wet because it would only stay on dry tarmac, and only that with practice.

"How do I get to Mossmorran on wet days?"

"Get yourself into a carpool and keep an eye on the weather forecast."

Billy was in a negative mood, and was always impossible to deal with when like this, he just looked for problems, so Anthony had decided just to ignore everything he said from now on. This was a shame because he was making some valid points. "So I say to some of the lads, let's get a carpool going. Do I tell them at this point that I have a two-seater with no doors or roof and that it only goes in the dry, or do I keep this to myself until I pick them up on the first morning it's my turn to drive?"

No response.

"I assume you can actually get insurance for home made cars."

Silence

"I smell burning, do you smell burning?"

Anthony gave up, "Look if you're going to be stupid about this let's just take it back." Then he changed his attitude suddenly as he noticed that a small fire was striving to become a blaze, and it was doing this just behind his head. It was coming from the golf ball holder, or boot to give it its official title as written on the scrap of paper that passed for a manual.

It took less than three minutes for the car to become a pile of ash. Billy kicked the ashes into the gutter and set off on the long walk home. His brother Anthony wisely decided to walk in the opposite direction even though this took him up to his neck in a pond. If only it had been deeper, thought Billy.

He was left with £100 with which he bought a Renault 18. The car was warm, dry and luxurious compared to the Dutton, though judging the Dutton after only ever driving it for six miles was perhaps harsh. It may have been a great car, but sadly he would never know.

Working at Mossmorran proved to be tiring but rewarding. He drove 80 miles a day round trip and worked seven 12 hours days, followed by six 12 hour nights then a turn-around day before starting the cycle again. Apart from the required turn-around day between nightshift and dayshift there were no days off, unless you took them unpaid. Even unpaid leave was frowned upon because they wanted these sites up and running.

The forward plan appeared to be, instrument installation and calibration on the Shell site, upon completion of which twelve Instrument Technicians would be kept on for commissioning while the rest began installation and calibration on the Esso site. The whole job would last just over two years and the money to be made was phenomenal.

Each technician was paired with a permanent partner. Due to the large number of technicians you could not use names on the radio so each person had a designated call sign. Billy Hunt was Checking 9, his partner Jock Ritchie was Checking 12. Jock was a bad tempered Fifer and there were signs that he once had red hair, but it had long since gone, even though he was only about 30. Billy really grew to like Jock and the feeling appeared to be mutual, they were like good cop, bad cop, and had secretly hoped to gain those nicknames, but the general consensus went with prick and prat.

Dayshifts were busy because witnesses worked dayshifts. The witnesses would be called for when you had an instrument loop complete and ready to sign off. They would stand with their clipboard and ask stupid questions. Billy and Jock had a great system in place based on the fact that the witness could only be at one end of the loop. On a temperature loop for example, Jock would stand at the control panel where the gauge was and Billy would put roughly the correct input in for 25%. Jock would then say up a bit or down a bit until he got exactly 25% and Billy would note down what input to use when the witness arrived. They took readings for all possible inputs. If the witness chose the field end for the test it was even easier because Billy would apply the correct input and Jock would say the correct output no matter what the instrument gauge read. They would have been quicker just doing it properly but if they did that they would eventually come across a faulty instrument and have to either cheat without the expertise they had gained, or fix it, which would be a real pain in the arse. No, their way worked just fine.

At the beginning of a dayshift each team was given six dossiers, that is: six information packs on instrument loops. The dossiers contained all the information, settings and drawings for the loop.

Four completed, witnessed and signed off dossiers constituted an acceptable day's work. It was no challenge to get through four a day, but getting witnesses could be time consuming because they were thin on the ground. Billy and Jock eventually decided to just invent a witness called Blair Nimmo. To this day there are over 100 instrument loops at Mossmorran signed off by Blair, a man who never existed.

Nightshifts were reserved for remedial works, additional installations and other odd jobs. A nightshift took the form: start at 8pm, work like a madman until midnight, have something to eat, play cards for two hours, then off the bed in the laundry room.

For two years, nothing went wrong in Billy's life. Work was great, the money was great. He didn't have time to drink and Lanna Green was beginning to have doubts about her sexuality.

When both sites were up and running the two companies even offered Billy a job. He would be working with Haig and Ringrose a third-party contractor for much less money, but these were offers of long-term secure employment. Billy realised that maybe he was meant to be an Instrument Technician after all.

He was about to choose the Shell site when he saw an advert in the Daily Record for a job with BP. He was once again at a crossroads in his life, but it felt more like a roundabout.

Chapter 7

Equally Insignificant

On a moonlit night a man approaches a crossroads at the south end of Rosedale where Highway 8 intersects with Highway 1. A guitar rests on his shoulder. He stops at the crossroads and he looks at all his options. It is a metaphor. A presence joins him and after an exchange, the man with the guitar walks purposefully on, in possession of musical genius, but minus a soul.

A crossroads offers three new directions, and one previously trodden. It did not serve for Billy. He arrived at a roundabout between Falkirk and Larbert at 2am on a clear starry winter's night. He arrived on his motorbike but without helmet and leathers. For reasons he would never know he had got out of bed twenty minutes earlier and climbed on his Honda 400 four, in jeans and tee shirt. If you are going to do something life changing, at least try to look cool.

At the roundabout he pulled over, leaned his bike on its stand and walked to an area of wasteland 20 yards distant. He lay on his back, never feeling the cold and stared at the sky. A moon, maybe Jupiter and a whole load of stars. How many stars? An infinite number.

He had bought a telescope two months ago, but had never considered looking at distant objects in the sky; he bought it to look at distant girls without being arrested. Unfortunately he bought a reflective rather than refractive type and consequently all the girls were upside down, this telescopic flip didn't matter when looking at stars and planets, but was a real problem when viewing girls, especially for someone who didn't understand their bodies even when they were the right way up.

On this night he used just his eyes but as no one was around afforded himself the luxury of putting his glasses on.

Like anyone who looks skywards and thinks, he was immediately struck by the enormity of it all. He was overwhelmed by the thought of the distances involved. Two stars which looked adjacent might be billions of light years apart. There was just no way to tag measurements to what he was looking at. He imagined if you looked long enough and thought hard enough; insanity would take hold in no time.

He wanted to know where he was, where he fitted into the whole scheme of things, the meaning of life question just wasn't pertinent enough, he wanted to know much more than that.

As he lay there he began to try and equate the span of his existence, possibly 80 years at best to the span of it all. Billions upon billions of light years. He thought of his life span in terms of being 1mm and wondered how and where that fitted into infinite.

It slowly came to his mind how completely insignificant he and his time on earth was. He tried to relate the distance between his significance and someone else's significance and then how close they would be in the context of infinite. There would be no gap that could be measured. He then thought of the most significant figure to have spent his time on earth at the same time as himself. Liberace, he thought. He's probably the most significant man of my time. Why he thought of a fat, sequined poof is a matter for a different debate, but he was getting close to understanding what he came to learn.

What he understood was that nobody mattered; nobody would put a scratch on the surface of entirety that could be seen or would need to be seen. Everyone would come and go and nothing of impact to the universe would be recorded.

Everyone is equally insignificant.

Once he realised this, he feared no one, respected no one, liked no one and disliked no one. Ships that pass in the night just couldn't do justice to his newly formed views on the interaction of insignificant people who shared with him his 1mm of eternity.

He climbed back on his bike and headed home. That's when he first felt the cold, he wished he'd put a jacket on. He got to Lathalan roundabout and veered towards Linlithgow, that's when he heard the siren, he wished he'd put a helmet on.

The insignificant policeman who took his details asked what he was up to. Billy tried to explain the man's insignificance to him but this didn't go down well and he ended up in a cell for the night.

While he fully understood the knowledge he had gained through this experience, he did concede that he might need to find a better way to explain it to others.

And so for Robert Johnson it had been a crossroads, for Billy Hunt it had been a roundabout. The difference was Billy still had his soul. He also had a £15 pound fine, but that wasn't significant.

Chapter 8

"Will You Marry Me?"

It wasn't as simple as just writing off for an application form when the company involved was BP. Billy had done OK at Mossmorran, not only had he been happy, his self-confidence had risen, and for the first time he seemed to be appreciated. Applying for a job with BP presented closets full of ghosts, did he really want to open that door?

What if communication lines were opened between BP and Shell or Esso, would that be bad? It would be bad he felt and on that basis alone he decided not to apply for the job.

As days passed, Billy could not get BP out of his head. In his heart he really wanted to work for BP again, it was like family to him. Yes they'd had their problems but that's what made them like family. They had gone through thick and thin together. He needed a sign, something to suggest to him that BP also wanted him but were holding back, through pride, from letting him know.

After several more days Billy decided he would need to initiate actions which would enable both parties to move closer together through fate. He got out his lucky coin. Before tossing a coin which may decide an important issue It is important to establish protocols and rules. Billy did this and even wrote them down so there could be no confusion.

Heads, he should apply. Tails he should not apply. The coin would be tossed seven times with majority outcome final.

He polished the coin then began tossing.

Tail, tail, tail, head, tail, head and finally tail.

It worked, he had a result of 5-2 in favour of him not applying today, and he could not wait for tomorrow's result. This was a good way to decide things; he wondered why nobody had ever used it before.

He should make plans. What if he got a positive result and did not have an application form to hand. He didn't want to do this thing in a half-baked manner. When fate is involved in decision making you have to be prepared to act on its fickle nature at a moment's notice.

He wrote in response to the advert and his application form arrived two days later. Fortunately the results prior to its arrival had been 6-1 and 5-2 in favour him not applying. Another 3 days passed, 5-2, 5-2 and 4-3 against. The closing date for applications to be submitted was looming so Billy decided he would complete the form and put a stamp on it so he could act quickly if need be.

By the time the last day for posting the form arrived Billy had lost faith in fate which had for over a week produced consecutively negative results. He didn't want to not apply but he did need a sign.

He decided to ask his father's advice. "BP has a job in the paper, do you think I should apply for it?" Billy's father was adamant that he should not apply but agreed to look at the newspaper advert which Billy had cut out.

"Have you actually read this Billy?" he asked. Billy admitted he hadn't looked at it in any detail, he had just seen that BP was looking for tradesmen including Instrument Technicians. "Let me read it to you then."

"BP Petroleum Development has a number of vacancies for time-served Instrument Technicians, Electricians and Mechanical Fitters. Successful applicants will be self-motivated and experienced technicians with a background in the Petrochemical industry; they must also have the ability to work within a team."

This was bad. Why should he work for a company which expected him to motivate himself and then share credit for anything he did? What if he did really well and got promoted to a supervisory post? What would his job actually be if everyone was going around motivating themselves?

His father continued. "Successful applicants will take up positions at Solheim Inlet in The Falkland Islands early in November."

It's in a fucking war zone, thought Billy. He would be dodging mines and snipers bullets making it difficult to focus on even the simplest calibrations. No, the coin had saved him.

"Successful applicants will benefit from a generous relocation package which includes subsidised housing, free trips to UK Mainland and a substantial settling in allowance."

Then again, the war was over and all the Argentines had returned home. It is quite likely that any unexploded mines would be well off the beaten track, where he would never need to venture.

"Dad, what does Solheim mean?"

"It's a Norse word meaning sun, so the location is a sunny inlet."

A sunny inlet, that sounded quite nice actually. "What do you know about the Falklands dad?"

"Not much really. It's a sheep farming community and also has penguins. I only really know what I saw on the TV when we were bombing it. Remember when we went on holiday to Germany?"

"Yes."

"Well you really liked Germany didn't you?"

"Yes."

"Well we bombed Germany and it seemed to make it a good place so I would imagine bombing the Falklands has had much the same effect."

"If your argument is true, why have we never bombed Bo'ness?"

Father and son went into raptures, ten years of conflict, lies and hurt were forgotten in a moment of bonding. All the emotional damage was repaired and they would never be parted again.

"Right, I'm off to the Falklands then," announced Billy.

This was not a statement of fact, more an optimistic wish. First he would need to apply, then he would need to be interviewed, then—and only then—he might get offered the job. A quick reality check made all this seem very unlikely.

Having said that, within a week of posting his application off, Billy had been invited to attend an interview at The Thistle Hotel in Glasgow.

He arrived at the hotel looking smart in his brother's suit and trying to look confident. It seemed deserted and he was asked to sit down in the reception area and await a call. After only a few minutes, a tall red-headed, red-bearded Scotsman introduced himself as Tom Hamilton and invited Billy to follow him to 'somewhere a little quieter'.

"Well Billy, how are you? You look smart; you needn't worry about this being too formal, I just want to have a chat with you before we get you packed off to Solheim Inlet."

"My goodness sir, you certainly know how to put the condemned man at ease, you speak like I already have the job," joked Billy.

"You do."

"Sorry."

"You do already have the job. I just need to get to know you a bit before we make the offer official," explained Tom.

"Wow, this is like no other interview I've attended, so I have the job, wow."

"Indeed you do young Billy. Now, are you married Billy?"

"No. Are you proposing?" Billy entered into the light-hearted proceedings, "I'm not gay by the way, that was just a joke," suddenly feeling the need to add some weighty ballast to the proceedings in case they floated off somewhere.

Tom Hamilton looked hurt, "I'm gay. You're not a homophobe are you Billy?"

"My god no, I'm straight as a dye. No offence meant, sorry. Live and let live I say. My ex-girlfriend is gay."

Hamilton sucked in sharply, "Ooh, that's got to sting a bit."

"Well, yes just a bit."

"Anyway Billy. Get married. The settling in allowance is £5000 for married men, £2500 for single men. Get married. Married men get a three-bedroomed house, single men get a one-bedroomed flat. Get married. Married men get two fully-paid trips home a year, single men get one. Get married. You see where I'm coming from here young Billy. Oh, did I say, get married."

"I'm half way down the aisle Tom."

"Good man, Billy Hunt. Remember ..."

"Get married?"

"Smart boy, well done. How do you feel about sheep, young Billy?"

"Sheep? I like a bit of lamb on a Sunday evening."

"Ever shagged or had the urge to shag one?"

"Fuck no," Billy was astounded but quickly regained control, "sorry Tom, I mean no, I would never, could never do that, no."

"Good man Billy Hunt. The reason we are putting in a domiciled workforce is to replace a contract workforce who for the most part have taken to shagging the local livestock population. Image, Billy, BP's image. Not good to have your men shagging the local livestock in a small community. It leads to jealously, resentment, unrest."

"Jealously?"

Tom thought about it. "Well, resentment and unrest at any rate."

The word jealously wandered around Billy's head, banging off the sides like a fly flying into glass thinking it could get out. No, the thought of people being jealous about people shagging sheep was never going to get out, that one was stuck there for life.

"Now do you have any questions for me Billy, before we sign the old contract and get you shipped off to the Falklands."

"Yes Tom. I'm sure this won't happen but what if my lovely wife decides not to join me in the Falklands until a little later?"

"Quite alright Billy. All you need is a wedding certificate and Pandora's Box will open before you."

"That's a relief, I think she may want to settle up things at home here in the UK before joining me," reiterated Billy.

"Well we'll get the papers out to you and tell you what you need to know to prepare and move to the Falklands in, shall we say six weeks? What's your fiancées name by the way?"

"Lanna."

The two men shook hands on the deal and Billy Hunt left feeling like the local sheriff getting his gun back. He was in the BP family again where he belonged.

"Hi Lanna, can you meet me in the Star at lunchtime, I have a proposal to put to you."

"I'd love to, as long as it's not a proposal of marriage."

"Well it's funny you should say that, see you about one in the back room."

Billy arrived early, he had to go over the words in his mind, and they had to be right because if he got them in the wrong order Lanna would just run away. He reckoned he had to get the whole plan across in one sentence, and then repeat the most important points in a second sentence. She would be on her feet by then so it had to be sharp and to the point, she just had to understand what he was proposing here.

Lanna arrived looking lovely. She had her top three blouse buttons undone to show him what he was missing, something she always did when meeting him. It was strange how she seemed to want to punish him for her decision to become a lesbian. Maybe it was his fault, she certainly seemed to take a 'you've ruined my life' attitude towards him.

"I didn't ruin your life by the way." Oh dear, he had developed a nasty habit of speaking what he was thinking.

She suddenly did up the buttons and said, "Sorry, I know you didn't."

This was such a weird moment. It's the first time he had ever understood a girl's motives, she really did undo the buttons to have a go at him. Wow, this needed to be looked into, what a weapon. Did he suddenly understand girls?—if he did then life was going to get a whole lot better. He put these thoughts on the back burner as there were more important issues to be dealt with.

"Thanks for coming and thanks especially for the glimpse of cleavage. I'm going to say something a bit strange now which will be very clear when I'm finished but will sound like Armageddon has arrived when I'm half way through."

Lanna, put her hand on his and gave him a sympathetic look. "It's OK Billy, the answer is yes, I will marry you."

Billy looked at his glass, which contained orange juice. He had stopped drinking some months ago and since then only good things had happened in his life. Was drinking the cause of all his problems, surely not?

Lanna spotted his confusion and decided to help him along a bit. "Right, correct me anywhere I go wrong. You are moving to the Falklands and a relocation package is on offer. A single man gets x and a married man gets 2x."

"Bit weak on the old x and 2x as you will remember, you were laughing at me in class that day."

"Darling, I was laughing with you not at you, stop being so sensitive."

Darling? Laughing with me? Cleavage? 'I will marry you'? Right this was just too crazy. Everything she'd said in the last 2 minutes suggested she was fond of him, she had undone buttons to please him and she actually seemed to want to marry him. He might need to think about this and re-appraise some moments from his past. His whole life had started going wrong in Miss Lightfoot's maths class, had he misinterpreted one sign and his life had unravelled due to a technical error.

"Pay attention Billy, you're starting to think and that will only confuse you. To continue without the x's. You get twice as much money if you are married. So, we get married, not a problem, in fact I've booked the registry office for Tuesday. After 6 months has passed we get the marriage annulled on the grounds that it has not been consummated."

"Eaten?"

"No, not eaten, not consummated means we haven't had sex during the first 6 months of marriage so all bets are off, no money or property exchanges and we walk away as we were the day before we married."

"That's what I was going to say. How did you know all this?"

Lanna sighed, "Because you've got a big mouth and you told my brother the whole sorry story in this very room last night."

"Oh, right, got you. Anyway, what do you think?"

"It's a good plan Billy. I like it. I like the idea of you getting, how much did you say it was?"

"I didn't and that's none of your business."

"OK, speaking of business, let's sort out the details. I want £500 cash, a new dress and a new hairdo. I want to look my best for you on the day."

"Can't your dyke, I mean girlfriend, I mean friend, sorry, can't she do your hair?"

"Nope, posh hairdresser, £50 hairdo, £50 dress, oh and I might as well have some shoes while we're at it. We'll call it £650 cash, up front, payment to be received before the happy day on Tuesday."

"We'll call it £600 total and you better not be late. What time is it anyway?"

"Two o'clock at the town hall."

Billy was in a daze. He wasn't sure what just happened. He appeared to have got everything he wanted for about the price he had hoped to pay and he hadn't had to open his mouth hardly. Keeping his mouth shut might be worth keeping in mind for future events such as this. Not that he expected to embark on a sham marriage too often.

Lanna had one last thought as she got up to leave. "When he or she says, 'You may now kiss the bride,' will you want tongues with that?"

"How much?"

"£25."

"Can we play it by ear and see how I feel on the day?"

"Fine by me but I'll need warning and payment up front, I don't suddenly want to find your tongue in my mouth then have to fight you over the money later."

"Sounds fair, I'll tell you before we go in."

The wedding passed off without hitch. Bobby Locke was best man, though he was not happy that he could not make a speech. Billy explained that he could make a speech when he got home and tell him about it next time they met. Helen Isles was lady in waiting, and she looked beautiful on the day. Billy had had the briefest of flings with Helen some years earlier. He had gone to Blackpool with three friends, and on discovering Helen would be there at the same time they arranged to meet up. When they got home she went back to completely ignoring him. The logic seemed to be, it was OK to go out with Billy Hunt, just don't be seen with him.

It was great being married. It was so normal, it felt so right. He had to keep reminding himself that he wasn't really married in the conventional sense and it was just a business arrangement to get him the extra £2500 minus payment for Lanna. She was no match for him; she could have asked for £1000 and got it, silly girl.

On the Friday night after his wedding, he headed for his usual orange juice at the Star. He had just got comfortable when Helen Isles walked in and after getting a drink, joined him.

"I don't mind telling you Billy, you really hurt me."

"I hurt you?"

"Seeing you married to Lanna. I had always dreamed that one day we might ..." She lowered her head and began to sob.

Fucking hell, thought Billy. Am I living someone else's life for them while they are on holiday? I get married and within a few days I have another girl sobbing in her drink because it wasn't her.

"You're taking the piss right, my mates are all around the corner laughing aren't they?"

This seemed to turn sobbing into full blown hysteria and their table was starting to attract attention. This might, to onlookers, put him in a bad light. There was a time, when making a girl cry was the first step to a gun fight in the street. Happily such days were past, though it did still happen in parts of Glasgow apparently.

"Come on Helen; let's get you out for some fresh air."

"Can you take me home, my parents are away and I don't want to be alone right now."

Billy walked her home and by the time they arrived at her door they had somehow ended up with their arms around each other. He was invited in for coffee and by the time he had drunk it they had somehow ended up lying on the settee together. After a long heart to heart which made them both feel much better they had somehow ended up sleeping together.

This was great. Billy got up and headed for home a new man. A real man. He had never had casual sex before, it was brilliant, he must do this again, and soon, he loved it. No pre-match meal, no discussions of commitment, no 'next week I might let you touch the other breast'. This was awesome, why hadn't he done this before? He enjoyed a lazy Sunday before going to bed to think about all the girls he knew who might be up for a bit of 'casual'. Sadly the list was beginningless, but never mind, he was moving away anyway and he felt confident Helen would offer a second helping of this joy.

Early Monday morning he was awakened by the phone ringing and scrambled out of bed to answer it.

"You are a beast Billy Hunt. I hate you. We haven't even been married a week and you sleep with my best friend. You pig. I want a divorce."

"Hi, Lanna, nice one, you had me going there. What's new, and by the way, be careful what you say, it's an annulment, remember?"

A man's voice came on the line. "Mr Hunt, I am Mr Ford of Ford and Bannerman. I'm afraid your long suffering wife is too upset to speak and has passed the phone to me."

"Long suffering wife? Wait a minute now; you don't understand what is going on here. Lanna and I have ..."

"Mr Hunt, I understand perfectly and I urge you not to say anymore until you make arrangements for a solicitor to advise you."

"She's a fully paid up lesbian who agreed to marry me for £600 with a £25 option for tongues which I never took up by the way."

"Mr Hunt, please control yourself, you not only betray this poor child, you then cast aspersions on her sexuality and openly imply she is a prostitute. I must end this call now but I urge you to seek legal representation at your earliest convenience." Ford hung up.

Shit, oh shit. This is bad thought Billy. He didn't know what was likely to happen but he knew annulments were free, and divorces were expensive.

Had he said 'silly girl'? My god, she was way out of his league. Still, look on the bright side, he could go and see Helen for some casual sex to take his mind off it. He had his left shoe on but before he got the right one on the penny dropped. Casual sex wasn't as casual as he had first thought. Oh dear. This was bad. He had once read about something called a 'honey trap' but hadn't really understood what it was until this moment.

Billy could not wait to get out of the country and asked BP if he could start a little earlier. They told him that it would take the full six weeks to get all the paperwork sorted out so this would not be possible. They also told him they were glad that he had called because they had been contacted by Ford and Bannerman who had insisted that his £5000 settling-in allowance be frozen pending the outcome of a divorce settlement.

"Why?" asked Billy.

"Oh, it's quite normal when someone is leaving the UK and they have unresolved legal matters. Just a precaution, nothing to worry about."

"But that's not right, the Falklands are part of the UK and according to Margaret Thatcher always will be."

The kind nameless lady in BP house explained that the Falklands were still considered unstable, and Argentina might ask for a return match at any time.

Billy didn't bother to argue, he never won where Lanna was concerned. He almost wished they had worked out from the start because she was so much smarter than him and together they would have been pretty good. He secretly admired her ability to always beat him. That was until he discovered that the proceeds from his flat sale were also being frozen.

Chapter 9

Over Egging the Pudding

Within two months he had relocated to his new home on the Islands.

His furniture and possessions travelled down on the same boat so he only stood in an empty house for a couple of hours before the removal men pieced his life back around him.

The house was detached and had been assembled from good quality portacabins, measurements suggested five. You would not know this if you looked at it from outside because it stood proudly as a Scandinavian-style country retreat. He liked it. Perhaps a bit too big for one man but bedrooms did not have to remain bedrooms. He envisaged one bedroom, a smaller music room and an even smaller study. He did not have any particular reason for a study but it just sounded like a good thing to have. If his parents phoned he could put them on hold and tell them he would take it in the study. The Billy Hunt image would be that of a 'single' man doing well. This is what Margaret Thatcher wanted and she was almost always high on the list of people to please. He simply adored the woman despite the hardship she had caused him in the early 1980s, which wasn't really her fault. After all it was The Tebbit who told him to get on his bike. Billy felt the man was a loose cannon who acted alone and for his own motives.

His relationship with Margaret was a strange one. After all she was a very strong and dominant woman and he was a control freak, not a match made in heaven, but her poster was the first one to stick to a wall in his new home. It went above his bed so she could inspire his dreams.

David Bowie had not replied to a single letter from Billy Hunt but Margaret Thatcher had replied to every missive, possibly not in person but at least someone had done it, and he was only one vote, but to her or her office he mattered. Being in the Falklands was perhaps his way of saying thank you and in some small way, his very presence on her battlefield was showing respect for her efforts.

Billy had three days to look around and settle in before he would start work. Three days was just a bit too generous. He had covered everything by lunch time of his second day as a 'Kelper'.

With its treeless landscape, never-ending winds, and the 110 uncleared minefields, it offered a spartan existence, better suited to a monk than a young go getter. Billy could not do anything about the wind but if he was going to be here a long time he might think about planting a few trees to make it more like home. That could wait though. A local shop keeper had brought up the subject of the mines and this was an immediate concern. He wrote to the local government office suggesting these ought to be dug up and thrown in the sea at their earliest opportunity. He wondered if someone from a well run town like Linlithgow might be able to play a role in local politics. His second letter was to the local broadcaster, he asked them which way he should point his TV aerial as his could not pick up a signal.

The postal service was excellent but the news was not. He received two replies the very next day.

"Dear sir, we are currently awaiting a response from the Argentine government to a request we made late last year for information on mine locations and numbers."

"Dear Sir, we have no television broadcasts in the Islands at this time and no plans are in place to bring television to the islands in the foreseeable future. You are however, able to watch video recordings if you have the correct equipment. You might also like to tune into local radio which broadcasts a fifteen-minute news program every second Wednesday at 7pm"

To be fair, the Daily Record brochure had not mentioned these things and neither had gay Tom. Both had to the best of his recollection mentioned the sun though and that was nowhere to be seen. In fact it was summer and it was fucking freezing. Rain, which was in great evidence was of the sideways variety, driven by the constant wind which blew it across the Islands before turning around and blowing the same rainwater back again before it ever reached the ground.

The most pressing issue was the lack of television. When he left Old Blighty two nurses had been taken hostage in Brookside Close. He had considered postponing his departure pending an outcome to the siege but this had not been practical and anyway he was sure he'd learn the outcome on his travels or soon after his arrival. The outcome was now something he may never know and this irked him more than a little.

Thirteen of the thirty new employees resigned before even getting a security photograph taken.

Billy considered joining them on the return boat trip but his life wasn't that simple. If he returned to Scotland he would inevitably get personally involved in his divorce from Lanna. If he knew one thing, it was, that not getting involved in anything to do with Lanna was the best option. Also, he had received a call from Helen on the day of his departure which suggested there might be happy news on the horizon. Any news which others suggested would be happy for them was almost always unhappy for him.

On the eve of his first day at his new job, Billy sat in his favourite chair looking at his switched off telly and sank into depression. He had not realised how important television was to him, just another thing he had taken for granted. He suddenly sat forward, struck by a thought. He had lost track of days, maybe even months, and may come to lose track of years, but one thing he knew was that he started work on Thursday. He therefore deduced that this was Wednesday and the fact it was dark outside did not necessarily mean it was night; it was dark 24/7 in this god-forsaken place. Maybe if this was an alternate Wednesday the news would be on the radio. He searched his packed crates for a radio, he had not felt the need to unpack this yet. There it was. Having no idea what frequency the program would be broadcast on he just sat and twiddled the knob back and forth and hoped for a voice to break through the static at some point. It seemed like an eternity passed, then suddenly …

"This is the fortnightly Falkland Islands news round up …"

Fuck me he thought, it's on once a fortnight and they still feel the need to round it up."

"… Mrs Caulton has decided to extend post office opening hours from next month. The post office will now be open on Tuesdays between 2pm and 3pm. Current opening hours; 2pm to 3pm on Fridays will not be affected by this change. Mrs Caulton said, 'We get so busy on Friday's now that we can hardly cope.'

"Bryon Caulton of Goose Green discovered a suspicious looking object on grounds belonging to local landlord Ian Caulton, last Thursday. Bomb disposal was called in to examine the object and ascertain whether it was a landmine left behind by the Argentine scum…"

Forgive and forget then, thought Billy.

"… but it turned out to be a very oddly shaped stone. The stone was made safe before being taken to the Stanley oddly shaped stone museum where it will go on display when the museum reopens to visitors next June.

"Little Toby Caulton has once again caused a stir in Fox Bay East by throwing stones at the postman. Mrs Caulton, Head Post Mistress refused to comment on this latest outrage but in private she is believed to be quite cross about the whole thing. Toby was in trouble only last year when he not only threw stones at the postman, 83-year-old Tommy Caulton, but also let the tyres down on his Land Rover. Tommy Caulton was unavailable for comment as he had a doctor's appointment to have his in-growing toe nail dressed. We did however catch up with Dr Caulton who said the toe nail and consequent wound were not healing well due to the patient's alcoholism and the fact that he smoked heavily."

The rules of doctor–patient confidentiality obviously worked differently on the bottom side of the globe, thought Billy, making a mental note not to consult the doctor about his thrush.

"In Darwin last night there was a large turnout of people who climbed a small hill just outside the village to kick an Argentine soldier's body which had been found on Monday morning. The soldier, whose identity has not been established was then weighted down with rocks and thrown into the sea. George Caulton who attended the ceremony told us it had been a very good event and that Cynthia Caulton had provided tea and cakes in the local hall afterwards."

Mental note, in the words of Basil Fawlty, 'Don't mention the war.'

"Finally, disturbing news just in, Jim Caulton's prize ewe was sexually assaulted last night. Constable Caulton attended the crime scene and said that investigations were at an early stage but he expected to arrest one of the new BP recruits very soon. That's all for this bulletin, we look forward to being with you again in a fortnight where we will be talking to Constable Caulton about his arrest and will also provide an updated weather forecast for January to April 2008."

That was great thought Billy. It's a lively little place this. He had learned more in 15 minutes than he ever could have if he'd read any of the books on the Falklands, which he had intended to but never got around to. That little Toby Caulton is a nasty piece of work, better keep out of his way he thought. A bit bleak on the weather front too, the implication was that they weren't expecting it to change any time soon.

He lay in bed that night thinking of happier places and times, like his cell in Saughton prison.

He arrived for work nice and early expecting a day of induction. Apparently this had been the plan but the plan had changed. Sergeant and Constable Caulton met them at the gatehouse and explained that the human resources department had postponed their plans for the day. Instead they were taken to a meeting room where Sergeant Caulton explained that they would be questioned over an incident they may or may not have heard about on the news last night. The incident related to the assault of Mr Jim Caulton's prize ewe and was of a sexual nature.

"Those of you who are married and will be able to provide evidence of their whereabouts on Tuesday evening from a spouse or child may go home now," said Sergeant Caulton. "Please report for work tomorrow, as you have today."

Those who are single or who cannot provide testimony as to your whereabouts on Tuesday evening please remain here and be patient. We will talk to you all and try not to detain you any longer than is necessary."

Billy clearly sat in the 'stay here' camp. He was not overly disappointed as it happened because if he had to go home he would need to find something to occupy his mind and that may prove difficult.

Only seven men remained behind. Billy sat for just over 2 hours, and saw three men called through a door, into what he assumed was another meeting room, before he was summoned.

As the interview progressed it wasn't so much, good cop bad cop, but more talking cop and silent cop, with Constable Caulton taking the non speaking role.

"You are Billy Frederick Hunt, born 6th June 1961 in Colchester formerly residing at 224A Linlithgow High Street, now residing at Upper Lea, Stanley, where you have lived for less than one week."

Billy had forgotten that his middle name was Frederick; having had neither desire nor cause to remember. He sat quietly waiting for Sergeant Caulton to proceed but then realised he was meant to answer the opening statement.

"Sorry, yes, spot on. Well done with the Frederick bit, I think it might be my middle name but I haven't heard it used since my christening."

Sergeant Caulton did not acknowledge Billy's compliment, or sarcasm, on the force's research; in fact the comment appeared to irritate him. "What time is it Billy?"

"I'm not sure, after eleven I guess."

"I notice you have no watch, would you care to look at this one?" Sergeant Caulton pulled up his sleeve to reveal his watch.

"Not bad," said Billy, "11:15 nearly. I wasn't far off."

"Would you like this watch back Billy, it's a nice watch."

The word back was the odd one out. It didn't fit in the sentence because it implied it was his watch. He pointed out to Sergeant Caulton that the watch was not his and asked if it had any significance. Sergeant Caulton told him it had been found near where the crime had taken place.

Billy, being a huge fan of Columbo felt the need to ask why the policeman was wearing evidence instead of presenting it to him in a tagged up plastic bag.

This didn't go down well. "You would tell me how to do my job Mr Hunt?"

"No, not at all, sorry. It's just unusual. I wonder if I might see the watch officer. Perhaps it might be useful if I held it myself."

To his surprise he was given the watch and he decided to give it a good Columbo examination before it was taken back. He studied it from every angle and took what information he could from it.

"Seen enough, Mr Hunt? Do you think I might have the evidence back?"

"Officer, can I make one or two observations about your evidence?"

Sergeant Caulton thought for a moment then decided that Billy could make his observations, nodding approval. A quick glance toward Constable Caulton told Billy he did not possess nodding rights either.

"It has a leather strap not a metal one." Billy held it out for both officers to show them the strap. "The fourth hole from the end is the one that has been clearly used for attaching the watch, you see, it is worn. My first point would be that if I put the watch on," he began putting it on, "I would need to put the pin through the 5th hole, like so, not the fourth. We can therefore assume that if this belongs to the criminal his wrist is slight thicker than mine, but not much."

Both policemen looked aghast, but allowed him to continue, permission given by double nod, suddenly the stiff was drawn into the farce, no doubt through excitement at learning something not in the Falklands Police Manual.

"The man you are looking for has or had a wife called Ruth and was probably married in 1970. Finally, I don't know if this helps, but he's called Stephen."

Sergeant Caulton looked disgusted, "You are either pretending to be psychic or taking the piss."

"Or I might be reading the back of the watch which says, 'For 10 happy years Stephen, love Ruth, and then the date 11th August 1980 is inscribed."

Now nobody likes a smartass and Falklands' finest plod were going to be no exception if the way he was hurried from the room was anything to go by. In a small community, making a fool out of anyone is not recommended but making a fool out of a police sergeant in front of his subordinate was sure to have repercussions. Billy would have to hope for the best but with a low crime rate he wasn't overly optimistic that this exchange would be forgotten in a hurry.

Billy's dealings with law enforcement in the past could be the subject of a book and one day might be. He returned home, made a cup of coffee and sat back to relive the edited highlights.

Match one. Billy and Neal Smith aged 14 had stolen and then hidden a paperboy's bicycle. After a week, they took the bicycle to the police station, said they had found it and handed it in. The next two visitors to the Hunt household had been Sergeant Ross, who openly expressed his doubts about the version of events given and the paperboy's mum who gave him £2 as reward for finding her son's bicycle. Billy Hunt 1, Police 0.

Match two. Billy and Jackie Morgan had broken into the West Lothian Cricket Club clubhouse. They took diluting orange juice which they drank undiluted making themselves sick. They also made off with four bags of crisps—assorted flavours—and a cricket stump. A lady walking her dog had seen them exit the premises and was able to identify Billy but not Jackie. Not identifying Jackie was not a problem because after 25 seconds of intense interrogation Billy finally succumbed, confessing all. Billy and Jackie were both given a stern lecture and no more was said about the matter. A hollow, as he was not charged, but technical, as he was caught, victory for plod. Billy Hunt 1, Police 1.

Match three. Anthony, his elder brother had purchased a moped for £8. On the night before bonfire night Anthony and Billy had travelled the length and breadth of Linlithgow setting light to every bonfire they could find. The count was in the teens. On bonfire night itself, while everyone was standing around a small campfire setting off fireworks, Anthony and Billy were cruising on the moped, which had only one seat, so Billy was precariously perched on the rear carriage rack. They were pulled over by police, who at one point had to return to their car for an extra notebook. Anthony's haul was, riding without licence, helmet, insurance, road tax, and carrying a passenger on a single-seated machine. Billy only managed no helmet. Both were questioned about the early lighting of bonfires but it was then realised that no such offence existed on the statute books, so it was forgotten about. Anthony copped for all charges except carrying a passenger when he convinced the police that he had not been aware of Billy climbing aboard. Had the police even bothered to check the performance degradation of a Puch Maxi 50cc moped when given an additional 10-stone load, they might have realised that Anthony was not telling the truth. They did not check; and in the end both brothers received a written warning from Sergeant McKenzie, a friend of their father's. For Billy this could be classified a no scoring draw. Billy Hunt 1, Police 1, with everything to play for.

Match Four. Billy was charged with urinating in a public place and wilful damage to the property of others. This was an interesting test case as it turned out, because many aspects of law were learned from it. Having just got off the train from Edinburgh, Billy had left Linlithgow station and suddenly felt the need to pee. He went to the closest wall and as was his modus operandi he pee'd not against it but over it. Before Google Earth was invented it was difficult to locate places geographically and on the other side of this wall was The Star & Garter beer garden, where people were enjoying lunch. The wilful damage to property charge did not stand up because it was established that the embellished meals were not the property of those eating them until such times as they paid their bill. The public house, which still owned the meals was unwilling to pursue the matter for fear that having their meals urinated on would be bad for business. Billy received a caution for urinating in a public place but was able to once again lay claim to a draw. Billy Hint 1, Police 1.

During the half time interval, Billy had assessed where the police tactics were failing. They were constantly over egging their pudding and going for the perfect goal. Why did they not see that sometimes you have to win ugly with a goal deflected in off the defendant's backside? Arrogance, that was their problem, the arrogance instilled in anyone when they put on a uniform of authority.

Match 5. In 1980, Billy faced his first serious charge, one which could have life-changing outcomes if he did not beat it. Fraud is an ugly word whatever way you dress it up. Whether it involves millions of pounds or pocket money seems not to matter, the word has a stigma few other words can match. Billy and a friend Gordon Laird had found a way to legally make money through a road tax loophole. They would hang around scrap yards and whenever a newly-scrapped vehicle was brought in, they would see if it had a valid road tax disc. If it did they would take it, go to the post office and cash in any full months remaining on the disc. This could get them anything between £2 and £24. For reasons Billy never understood, a road tax disc not matching the registration of Gordon's Alfa Romea Sud ended up on the car. An eagle eyed, uniformed, traffic warden spotted this and called the police. Both friends were charged with fraud. It was obvious to anyone that Billy had done nothing illegal but despite this his lawyer advised him to plead guilty and then when given the opportunity to speak before sentencing he should tell his side of the story. Pleading guilty would put the judge in a better frame of mind and he would benefit from the wigged man's good will, it was thought.

If asked to list the best days in his life, appearing at Falkirk Sheriff Court would be in the top five. He was called late on in proceedings, so was able to sit back and enjoy other cases as they passed through. A man charged with drink driving had broken up with his girlfriend, then when leaving her house had got a puncture. His spare tyre was flat so he had gone into a nearby bar to call a friend for help. He'd had a pint while waiting, then his friend arrived; they got a good tyre fitted before both drove off. After travelling 100 yards he was stopped and 'bagged'. If he lost his license he would lose his job and his mother would throw him out making him homeless.

"Guilty, £30 fine, banned for 18 months."

This was great. A series of sob stories were told, the judge then imposed maximum sentence and people cried. The only thing that concerned Billy was that he was about to stand up and present a good sob story, this might be a problem if the judge stuck to form. As it happened, after telling the judge he had no knowledge of his friend's actions and was very sorry that he had unwittingly allowed an offence against her majesty to be committed, Billy closed his eyes and said a prayer.

"Mr Hunt, having listened to your explanation I have no option other than to change your entered guilty plea to a plea of not guilty. Are you happy to have your plea changed?"

Well, if you must, thought Billy. "Yes your worship, thank you."

"It's your honour."

"Thank you your worship."

Billy Hunt 2, Police 1.

Before he turned thoughts to the spectacular own goal that led to him serving time, thus levelling the match, the phone rang. This came as a complete surprise because he didn't know he had one. He followed the sound to the kitchen and found the source. "Hello."

"Sergeant Caulton here, do you own a green Land Rover registration FK 197?"

"No."

"Leave it lads, it's not his."

The match was moving into extra time.

Chapter 10

The Missionary Position

Like déjà vu, Billy did it all again the next day, arriving bright, early and keen. After being shown into the meeting room where induction would be held he did a quick head count. Sixteen men, meaning the drop out had increased from the previously known thirteen to fourteen.

"Good morning gentlemen." Tom Hamilton had slipped into the room and was coming at them from behind, no doubt this gave him great pleasure.

He jerked his head around in different directions, obviously carrying out the same head count Billy had just completed. "I heard we'd lost another one. Only the valiant remain," he joked. "Yes, I heard this morning that Stephen Sneddon and his wife Ruth had left yesterday afternoon, never mind, we still have one spare."

"One spare?" enquired a bearded man who would later become Ralph Gordon.

"Yes, Ralph, is it?" Ralph nodded. "We recruited thirty of you with a view to losing fourteen in very short order. The order has been shorter than anticipated to be fair, but we still have one more than we need so we will have to treat sixteen of you well." The laughs never stopped coming with gay Tom on stage.

Although the word redundancy hadn't actually been uttered the implication was that they would be happy to lose a body at some point. This was the first time redundancy had ever been hinted at on Billy's first day. It was all very unsettling because the word redundant and the name Billy had appeared in the same sentence far too often in his life.

Tom caught sight of Billy. "Billy Hunt, did you get married son?"

"I did Tom, but my wife isn't able to join me at the moment, she will follow on soon we hope."

"Oh, have we lost one? You're a pretty boy from some angles, still, she might not turn up, eh?" The wink was worse than the word's. He might find himself fighting off a groping gay boss if he didn't watch his step. This had to be nipped in the bud. He wrote on his induction sheet, 'Nip Tom in bud.' Not the wisest choice of words but he knew what it meant.

The person sitting next to Billy put his hand up.

"This chap with his hand raised is John Michaels gentlemen. I don't know if you've had a chance to introduce yourselves to each other yet but on the assumption you haven't I will do the honours of sharing names at every opportunity. Yes John, you have something to say?"

"My name is John Marsden as it happens."

"Sorry John, thank you for correcting me."

"Tom, you said you had wisely built in a dropout rate and I must say you seem to have managed to get pretty close to the actual numbers. Can I ask how many instrument technicians, how many fitters and how many electricians you started with and how many you planned to end up with?"

"Simple one that John, ten of each dropping to five of each."

"How many of each trade make up the sixteen of us here I wonder," mused John.

Tom looked irritated by this Marsden musing but felt it might actually be a useful exercise to see where they stood on useful numbers as opposed to numbers. "Gentlemen, a show of hands please. Instrument lads raise hand—ten; fitters raise hand—six; electricians raise hand—no hands. I just need to nip out and see someone so if you could chat among yourselves and get to know each other I won't keep you waiting long."

Tom was actually gone for three hours and during this time everyone took the opportunity to introduce themselves to the group and look for a clique to join.

The returning Tom looked markedly less stressed than the one who had departed. "Sorry lads, bit of business needed attending to. Before we crack on with the induction I think we should take lunch. Iain Bennett, a colleague of mine, is going to join us after lunch and will talk to you about the multi-skilling elements of your new job."

"Multi-skilling?" This statement not easy to attribute to any one person as it seemed to come from every seated mouth in the room.

"Yes gentlemen, lunch, see you back here in 30 minutes."

After a bite to eat the new recruits headed for the coffee lounge where Sandy McClure went around asking each person if they were an instrument technician or a fitter. Having gathered the ten instrument technicians into a group he announced his credentials as a former shop steward and asked if anyone had any objections to him hastily taking on the role of spokesman, a buffer between men and management. No objection was forthcoming so he leaned back slightly and hooked his thumbs behind his collar. This immediately gave the men confidence and confirmed to any doubters that he was experienced in handling employer–employee disputes.

"Lads when we return to the meeting room five of us are going to be told to convert to electricians. Does anyone here doubt that?" No doubters emerged. "Are any of you happy to undergo a swift and no doubt ill-planned-for conversion from one who pokes around with 24v dc to one who pokes around with a voltage that if mishandled will blow you to Chile and possibly beyond.?" No willing poke converters emerged. "Then gentlemen, at the first mention of retraining, I will rise to my feet and leave the room. I expect you all to follow me. Do I have your word that each and every one of you will follow me from the room?" Nine committed followers emerged and announced their emergence with a firm unambiguous nod.

Back in the meeting room Tom introduced a weasel faced Iain Bennett. Tom then sat down giving the floor to Bennett. "Gentlemen, congratulations on joining one of the most forward-thinking companies in the oil and gas business today. BP can offer you new horizons, new opportunities and a first insight into new industrial thinking. I doubt if any of you could have imagined for instance that BP is going to blaze the trail in multi-skilling opportunities for skilled workers. We will offer a retraining package to—"

As good as his word Sandy McClure rose and walked from the room.

Completely flummoxed by this, Iain Bennett broke off from his new world vision and looked at the fifteen men who remained before him. He picked out Billy and shrugged his shoulders saying, "What the fuck just happened?"

"During the lunch interval Sandy was sitting at my table and he mentioned he was having doubts and even suggested that he might resign. A number of us tried to reason with him but it seems we have failed, sorry."

"No apology needed son," interjected a protective Tom. "It's a shame but at least we have our numbers now, good news for the rest of you in a way, welcome to job security land lads."

The induction meeting progressed through the afternoon by the end of which four instrument technicians and the fitter least resembling a primate were asked to undergo electrical training commencing at 9am on Monday. Billy had escaped the retraining fate by suggestively batting his eyelids at Tom throughout the selection process.

The men learned what was in store for them over the coming weeks. They would each be paired with a newly redundant travelling status contractor who would train them in the workings of the oil terminal.

Graham Sinclair asked if the soon-to-be-unemployed contractors were comfortable with the idea of teaching their replacement the job. He was assured that it would be fine because the contractors had been offered a generous pay-off subject to their full cooperation in this very matter.

The oil terminal was divided into three areas, processing, known as process area; oil and gas distribution, simply known as distribution; and power generation which was known as utilities. Billy was assigned to the process area. John Marsden was also assigned to this area and they would join four other instrument technicians who already lived locally and were not therefore subject to the cull. When introducing themselves they used only surnames but added a number which was derived from their age. They were, Caulton 42, Caulton 35, Caulton 28 and Caulton 22. Billy asked if they changed their name on an annual basis which seemed to puzzle them, until they realised why he was asking. They explained that their number corresponded to their age on joining the company not their current age, so there was no need to change their name each year.

Billy then asked what would happen if another Caulton aged 22 joined the company, he was told this person would be called Caulton 22b and as it happened there was a Caulton 35 b and c in the utilities area. Finally he asked the more obvious question, was every Falklander called Caulton? No, he was told, but most were. Having sorted out the naming philosophy, the two new recruits questioned the Caultons on aspects of the job, the perks and island life in general. Without meaning to they had hit upon a contentious issue. The perks, they explained were non-existent for Falklanders whereas incomers got settling in allowances, subsidised housing and free trips home. John asked if this was likely to be a problem and Caulton 42 replied, "You bet, arsehole."

During their first weeks on the terminal John and Billy found the soon-to-be-redundant contract lads helpful and cooperative. This both surprised them and worried them. Leaving seemed not to be a problem for them; in fact they were at pains to get the new recruits up and running as soon as possible lest their departure be delayed.

Billy liked John; he was good company, liked a drink and also, he could be called upon for a frame of snooker any time, day or night. John's wife was also 'following on', so neither had any reason not to enjoy life to the full. He learned that John, who was a Geordie, had applied for the job after being persuaded to cross Scargill's picket line, an act which had made staying on mainland Europe difficult to say the least. "Do you feel safe here in the South Atlantic?" asked Billy. "I still sleep fully dressed with my running shoes on," admitted John.

Caulton 22 was making overtures toward possible friendship with Billy and John. They attributed this to his age and a consequent desire to here story's about life in the real world. Despite the fact that a local friend might be useful they ultimately dismissed his application for friendship on the grounds that he was too weird. He looked like the cavalier on a McEwans Export tin, which in itself was no big deal, but he was in their opinion, the stereotypical product of inbreeding on a massive and prolonged scale. His head didn't fit his body for a start and he walked as if a horse had kicked him in the nuts. This was a big deal and they told him so for his own peace of mind. When rejecting his friendship they hadn't known that Caulton 35 was his father and when the father took issue with their behaviour towards his son all they could say was, "So you were thirteen?" Caulton 35 reminded them that names were based on age when joining the company not current age and went on to say that for the record he had been 15 and Caulton 22's mother had been 12 when he was born. This cleared the matter up quite nicely and everyone moved forward in an atmosphere of greater understanding. "Don't even go for a piss with any of these cretins in the washroom," advised John.

Billy and John decided after about six weeks that they were missionary's bringing knowledge to an indigenous uneducated population. Thinking of their new life in this way helped them enormously in coping with life on the Islands. BP had a social club in Stanley where the new recruits could all meet and talk about their personal experiences of life and work on a rock in the middle of nowhere. The new team all seemed to get along fine and adversity gave them a strong bond.

With regards to the job, Billy was quite happy with things. The contractors had all left, so the place was being maintained by a mix of new recruits and local imbeciles. This offered Billy a status of assumed competence with his colleagues, a standing he had never previously enjoyed.

Two whole years passed relatively free of incident before opportunity knocked and Billy decided to answer the door. A vacancy arose for an instrument technician on shift. Such vacancies seldom cropped up because a shift job was regarded as dead man's shoes. The position was just too cushy and too well paid for anyone to resign it. The dead man in this case was Caulton 62 who had been with the company for 12 years. He had apparently passed peacefully in his sleep at home but his body was discovered by his day shift relief in the workshop. It was normal practice to carry dead employees onto the site as it had a significant impact on the life insurance money. Three times annual salary offsite, five times annual salary if the deceased expired on duty.

Billy attended the funeral as a mark of respect to the man whose job he intended to apply for. He took the opportunity to console the widow Caulton, a bubbly teenager with lips and hips to die for. "I'm so sorry at your loss Mrs Caulton. Had you been married long? I only met him twice but he was a lovely man. Your children will be a great comfort to you at this sad time. Did he owe any shift swaps?"

Caulton 62 as it turned out was owed two shift swaps, this was great news for Billy and made him determined that the job must be his, whatever it took to get it.

Having sent a lovely bunch of flowers to Tom Hamilton, Billy was duly interviewed and offered the job of 'B' Shift Instrument Technician. He was asked if he was familiar with the 'B' shift plant operators and was able to say that he had worked well with them as a day worker and expected to be a good member of the shift team. "They are a different bunch when the dayshift go home Billy," warned Tom. They would all get along fine Billy assured Tom.

The strange thing about 'B' shift was that none of the operators was a local, they had all moved from Shetland some years ago to take up positions on the Terminal. This on the face of it made them quite normal, many even talked about football and strip clubs during recess. He really looked forward to mixing with a better bunch of chaps with wider interests to share.

Chapter 11

'B' Shift

Talented, witty, inventive, cruel, caring, evil, loving, loathing, contemptuous, honourable, it's difficult to find the words to describe 'B' shift as collective, but as individuals these words pretty much cover the component parts.

Though the role was site-wide, Billy would rarely see the operators who cared for utilities because his role was to provide breakdown cover, and utilities seldom had breakdowns. On those very rare occasions it did the instrument technician would not be called because it was a very private place. Utilities were housed in an enormous tin shed and it sat upon a hill like a Gothic mansion. Inside the metal shed strange characters lurked, like 'early man'—an operator resembling Lurch from the Adam's family. The inhabitants made visitors feel so uncomfortable, they seldom returned. The sounds of the Gas Turbines lent to the shed an air of haunted mystery and evil.

In practice his remit was to potter around in the workshop when idle and dance to the tune of process and distribution operatives when they called upon him. If he was summoned by both areas at the same time he was empowered to prioritise. If his choice of client was disputed by the neglected party they could call upon the Shift Controller, John Robinson, who would decide the priority. As a shift controller, he could choose to relax and enjoy the trappings of power; he in fact rejected comfort in favour of moving among his people for the purpose of giving inspiration. While in his presence his men were mindful of his power but were able to relax because he was fiercely loyal to his children, like a parent he might scold them occasionally but if anyone else did, well Hell mend them.

The operators in process and distribution were a typical mix of keen ambitious, accepting, coasting and happy go lucky. Keen ambitious is a dangerous state of mind for anyone coming into contact with this badge holder. As a shift instrument technician, this breed represented the worst form of humanity. They would keep the technician busy because they, like him, also filled in a Shift Log. Good and proper use of the technician in pursuance of optimal plant operation reflected well on them. Accepting coasting operators were great they would never trouble anyone far less a technician who might want to involve them in his work. Happy go lucky, were the ones who made a 12-hour shift pass in less than what seemed a month, they were the fun element of working life.

The guys on 'B' Shift who Billy aspired to be friends with were tight, loyal to each other and extremely gifted in what they brought to the unit.

Bill Foster, who played guitar in a local band, aptly named Island, was not just a very good musician. His function on shift was paper-based. Anything to do with paper, you made an appointment with Bill. He held origami classes between 2am and 3am on Monday nightshifts. He was an expert in calligraphy so could make any certificate that might be required. He also altered shift logs and enhanced appraisals for a small fee. As a shift man your logbook is your method of passing on to the management and your shift colleagues what you did, why you did it and when you did it. Any suggested follow up would also be passed on through this legal document. Bill could save your career—even your life—when it came to the shift log.

This log is the best weapon in management's armoury but a most dangerous record for the person who wrote it. For example, 'Called to PT 201. Corrected zero error of 8%, blew down impulse lines, put back on line and working OK.' No problem there, the author attended, acted and made the situation good. Then two days later it is found that an isolation valve has been left closed on PT201, an Oil Tanker has received oil based on an incorrect calculation of pressure and the company is out of pocket by $44,275. Now the shift log is no longer a friend to the author, it is a stick to beat him with. In such an event Bill would be called in and after a little work the shift log and its carbon copy, that's worth repeating, and its carbon copy, would read. 'Called to PT201, instrument appears to be working but on investigation was seen to be dropping to zero after 12 minutes' use at operating pressure. Left Instrument isolated, could dayshift engineer please arrange to have instrument replaced prior to loading of "Tangiers Queen", which has projected arrival in 48 hours but no sooner."

Moving on. Ryan Leask was the brake on the runaway machine that was 'B' Shift. All non-conventional projects had to pass through him for approval because he was sensible and could spot a missing safety net under the tightrope. His job was to keep the lads out of trouble.

He was tall, handsome, well dressed and smooth. Strange gay Tom had never mentioned him thought Billy.

Andrew Williams was the inventor. Had Falklands been blessed with television at the time, the locals would no doubt have seen a programme called 'The Great Egg Race'. In this half-hour programme, teams would be given some glue, some plastic, a hose pipe and a camera. They would then have to create something that could fly to 100 feet, take a photograph of an 'X' on the ground, then land safely on an area of ground 1metre square enclosed by painted lines. Andy could do stuff like that, whatever contraption was required, he could make it using only a selection of bits from £45 million pounds worth of items in the BP stores.

Billy's first experience of Andy was after being called to distribution to look at a chart recorder which was apparently not recording. He arrived and asked where it was. Having been shown an empty slot in the panel where the recorder was meant to be, he joked, "That's why it isn't recording, it's missing."

The foreman, Ed Sutherland, who had no sense of humour, but was a good man despite that, sighed and said, "Can you get us one to put in there?"

Billy rushed to the workshop and got one, rushed back and fitted it, then accepted an invitation from Ryan Leask to partake of tea. While drinking his tea, Andy entered the control room, declaring "It's ready". He was carrying a strange assembly of parts which he placed on a chalked line on the floor. Billy noticed another chalked line about 6 yards further ahead.

"Right," said Andy. "Let's remind ourselves of the challenge. My 'buggy' when released will travel up to that line, stop on it, then reverse back to the starting line and stop on it."

Nods from those present accepted that this was indeed the challenge and wished him luck. Billy nearly fell off his chair when he saw the 'buggy' perform exactly as advertised. Once Andy had taken well earned plaudits, Billy examined the machine and it had all the parts of a Fisher Chart Recorder but assembled in a very different manner. To say Andy was a genius would be an understatement.

Bobby Mitchell was the distraction. A tall red-haired, red-bearded slim hippie. He looked odd and he acted odd, and that's what made him the distraction. His only function on 'B' Shift was to focus people's attention away from the reality of any situation. For example, the lads are having a game of cricket in the control room and Shift Controller John walks in to provide inspiration for his men. You could have a bowler, a batsman, a wicket keeper, fielders at slip, point, and mid-off. None of these would be seen by John because the moment he came through the door Bobby would set fire to himself and run from the control room screaming. John would chase him to put him out and by the time he returned, rain had stopped play, the covers were on and the players were all back in the pavilion. It's simple to draw attention to yourself, anyone can do that, but Bobby had timing and a 4th sense, he could draw attention to himself at a millisecond's notice without warning.

The final member of this extraordinary league of lunatics was Roddie Ratner. Roddie had no redeeming features, he was of average height, a bit over weight, stupid to the point of being an imbecile and though he claimed to speak English it was not a form of the language anyone seemed familiar with. His main weakness was that he was incapable of coherent thought and had no concept of cause and effect. To the group this was his main strength. He would hit anyone and anything they pointed at. He would hit it hard and always twice, never once, never three times, always twice. Once while the group was taking a stroll round the Tank Farm, Ryan Leask had mentioned a van parked precariously near the edge of the bund wall, only a yard away from dropping 50 feet into the bund itself. Andrew had said, "Where?" and without thinking Ryan had pointed at it. The next day the van was found, a total right off, sticking out of the side of Tank 07. The first hit had launched it down into the bund; the second had embedded it in the tank. Roddie was the perfect thug and a useful man to have on board.

Billy so much wanted to join this band of brothers but it wasn't an organisation you just asked to join, that would be seen as weak and pathetic and would have made him the target of ridicule. No, subtlety and planning would be needed. Find where they are lacking and demonstrate an ability to plug the gap.

His most obvious 'in' was via the gift of bullshit. They lacked it and he had an honours degree in it, then some. He would not bullshit them because they may feel threatened and may point at him. The bullshit would be presented in a wider forum, on a perfect stage. The team, if he had judged it correctly, would recognise it as bullshit and would be suitably impressed; all others present would fall for it, thus demonstrating its vital role in industry. There are times and places for the delivery of bullshit, the audience should be large and vulnerable, the time should be immediately after a meal when the senses were dulled, the stomach was happily digesting food, preventing the mind from digesting absurd information. An after dinner meeting fitted the criteria perfectly.

Thursday night shift ended the shift cycle, and preceded ten days' leave for the crew. The rule on a Thursday nightshift was to keep a low profile and do as little as possible. It was on a Thursday night at 9pm when the inspirational Shift Controller asked everyone to attend a pre- Gas Plant 2 start-up meeting. The Process area had two gas plants and after being shut down for planned maintenance they would always be started up on night shift to limit casualties if it all went horribly wrong. It was not a big deal starting up a gas plant but it was not a Thursday night wind down task in anyone's mind, save for management. The meeting was to be held at 1am in the Process Control Room and all operators and shift technicians would be required to attend. "Enjoy your meal and I'll see you all there," were John's instructions.

At 1am sharp, John called for everyone's attention. "OK lads, it's Thursday night so let's go on leave with a sense of achievement under our belts. Tonight we have been asked to bring Gas Plant 2 back online and we will start the procedures at 2am. I want everyone alert and on the ball; we should hopefully have everything up and running before breakfast. Any questions?"

Billy raised his hand and was invited to speak. "Thanks John. I just wanted to say that I did a bubble test before coming here ..."

"A bubble test?" enquired John.

"... yes, sorry a bubble test is something I often do if things are a bit quiet, it keeps me busy and lets me see how the plant is running as a whole."

"I'm impressed Billy, I have no idea what you are talking about but it's impressive."

Without knowing it John Robinson had just defined bullshit. Ryan Leask on the other hand, did know it and he sat forward in his seat and fixed his stare on Billy.

"Well, John, I'll give you the basics of what I did and what I found, you will find it interesting I'm sure. I went to LT201 and opened the drain valve ..."

"You never asked us for a permit to work on LT201," declared the keen ambitious Caulton39.

Ryan pointed at him and he immediately slumped back in his seat unconscious from two well directed blows.

Paper boy, Bill Foster, stood up, "Just to clear that up, I told Billy he could do a bubble test, I can show you the paperwork later if you want to see it."

"Not necessary, Bill, carry on Billy, you were telling us about your test."

"Yes, I drained some oil from LT201. Before running true, the oil came out in bubbles. It took 13 seconds to run with fluidity and an acceptable viscosity. Thirteen seconds tells me that the Ninja field is running at 95% efficiency and the Bravo field at between 84% and 88% efficiency. This gives us an oil ashore coefficient of 0.925 or certainly very close to it."

"Is that good?" asked John.

"Well it's good for normal running, but it's by no means ideal for a gas plant start up."

"Why?"

Bollocks! he was making this hard; still, the bullshitiar once started must never stop until he has 100% of his audience in the pen with the gate locked behind them.

"Well as you know John, . . ." (Always turn your victim's arrogance against him—Code 17, Sub-code 4) ". . . it tells us that a coefficient of 0.925 will mean water content of greater than 0.2% but not exceeding 0.45%, . . ." (Present figures as a percentage, shit, a mean percentage—Code 9, Sub-code 2) ". . . that's mean of course."

"Of course," nodded John as if his intelligence was being insulted, which it was.

"You start up a gas plant with those figures and, well I don't need to tell you the unnecessary cost that will be incurred," closed Billy with a knowing nod.

"Indeed, Billy. In light of this information I think we will be wise to postpone start up. You don't happen to know when conditions will be favourable for start up do you Billy, I mean I could do my own bubble test but as you've already done one ..."

"Tomorrow night is looking good John."

The meeting closed and everyone wandered off to their card game or bed depending on their level of commitment to the company. Billy made it as far as the car park when he was approached by Ryan Leask. "Pop over to distribution for a chat later Billy"

It was like that first 'accidental' brush of Lanna's breast, no other way to describe it, exhilarating, dangerous and tense. He was in.

Chapter 12

Preferred Lies

Every situation has positives and negatives. Billy was happy on 'B' Shift, he had been adopted by the 'in crowd', was earning excellent money and had more time off than he knew what to do with. And right there was the negative. Quite apart from having nowhere to spend his ever-increasing disposable income, there was simply nothing to do with his time. He was not alone; everyone on the islands seemed bored with the possible exception of Sergeant and Constable Caultons, who were always busy trying to fit him up for some misdemeanour.

Their best effort to date was a murder charge. Billy had apparently killed a tourist and disposed of the body. Though the alleged tourist had been reported missing by no one, though there was no record of his arrival in the Falklands by conventional means, though he clearly did not exist, it was a tough rap to beat. The police stated that it was a perfect crime because no evidence existed and it was unlikely that a body would be found. Any one not called Caulton realised it was the perfect non-crime but Caultons all were unanimous and vehement in their outrage that an 'incomer' would start murdering tourists. They depended on tourists, who generated £100s a year in revenue for the islands.

The case remains open to this day but no formal charges have ever been brought, this only thanks some quick thinking on the golf course.

Though the climate did not lend itself to a golf course, one had been created in a valley three miles outside Stanley. The course had 18 holes, 8 on one side of the steep valley, 8 on the other, even steeper side of the valley and 2 straight down the centre. Billy had never seen the course but when he was invited to join his new friend Ryan Leask in a game, he accepted without hesitation. It seemed like it might just be the thing to pass time away.

Billy and Ryan walked onto the first tee in bright sunshine, not a breath of wind, to help them shape their shots, was in evidence. Ryan hit his tee shot down into the right rough some sixty yards ahead of them and Billy followed suit, to be friendly. They battled into the sleet which was being driven painfully into their faces and arrived at their balls which were within yards of each other. Ryan lifted his ball, walked to the fairway with it and built a lovely little launch pad to sit it on.

Seeing Billy's confused look he said, "It's preferred lies in these conditions."

Before Billy had chance to lift his own ball, the sun was shining and the sleet shower had ceased as quickly as it had begun. "Bad luck Billy, play her where she lies."

After completing 18 holes Billy returned a score of 129 and Ryan just pipped him with a creditable 91. "It's not about playing the course here, it's about playing the conditions Billy," advised Ryan, "you'll soon get the hang of it."

It's about fucking cheating you mean, thought Billy, secure in the knowledge that he no longer had a problem with speaking what he thought.

Billy and Ryan would get to the golf course at every opportunity. It was towards the end of the six-week season when they had a game they would never forget. Both had started well sticking to fairways on holes one, two and three. Then on the fourth Billy went off piste right with Ryan favouring a wicked hook left. They parted agreeing to meet at the green sometime. Billy hacked forward in instalments, reaching the green seven shots later. He waited, no sign of Ryan. He waited some more, nothing; 20 minutes passed before he decided to leave the safety of the green and work his way down the side of the fourth he had last seen Ryan heading for.

"Here, Billy, over here," shouted Ryan in a deliberately muffled voice. "Look at this."

"What is it, oh fuck me, is that ...?"

"Yeh, it's a body, Billy."

"Is he dead?" asked Billy too squeamish to look.

"Oh yes, he's dead alright. Hey is this the tourist you murdered?"

"I didn't fucking murder a tourist Ryan, stop fucking about, what are we going to do?"

"He looks like a tourist," offered Ryan ignoring the pertinent question.

He did look like a tourist too. He lacked the survival kit that any person with knowledge of the course would carry. No thick jacket, woolly hat, woollen gloves, wellington boots, all standard Falklands' golfing kit. He also had an umbrella lying next to him which was like having a chocolate fireguard; umbrellas just blew away in this part of the world and were seldom used by locals.

"You're right Ryan, he is a tourist. This is not good for me under the circumstances. What do you think he died of?"

"A three iron I would say, see the angle of the groove in his forehead. I don't think he was struck down here though, see the shape of the wound, it suggests he's been hooked, so he probably died on one of the front nine sloping holes because they lend themselves to a hook. Go through them."

Billy for some reason saw sense in this approach and joined in the theory. "The first," he offered, "too near the clubhouse;" continuing, "the second is a par 3, no one would take a three iron out of the bag, the hole is too short."

"Right." Ryan approved. In perfect counterpoint they said, "The third." Yes it had to be the third. It was nearby, it couldn't be the hole they were on, it was too flat and few people hooked an iron off tee or fairway on this hole. Wait a minute though, "Ryan, you hooked your tee shot." After a moment's pause, "Driver Billy, I hooked a driver." Good point well made. It had to be the third.

Perhaps it was the shock of finding a body but after congratulating themselves on their detective work it slowly dawned on them that none of this actually helped them or hinted at what they should do next.

Ryan was first to accurately appraise the situation. "Look, sorry to say this Billy, but what we have here is a dead tourist and that is a commodity you more than anyone do not want turning up while the murder investigation is still an open file. I say we have two choices here, call the authorities and you say goodbye to liberty for 20 years or get rid of the fucker."

Billy was moved. He and Ryan were friends but not lifelong buddies or little boys in a Rolf Harris song. That he would help Billy out of a bad mess, not of his own making, but a bad one all the same, well he could have hugged his friend and fully intended to after making a short speech, "Ryan, you are a true friend and I—"

"Fuck off, Billy, I'm not doing this for you, I just spotted his clubs."

A brand new virtually unused full set of Ping Irons, complimented by three Hippo metal woods and a Seve Ballesteros precision weighted putter lay six yards downstream of Ryan's pointed finger.

This was not a time to appraise motives, this was a time for disposing of a dead body and both set to work thinking how this might best be achieved.

"Get your scorecard out Billy."

"I haven't putted out at the fourth yet, I was waiting for you, I got there in three though."

"No, forget scoring, write down ideas on the back, I will do the same. We put them together and any ideas that coincide must be good ones, we'll pick the best. Remember, leaving the body here is not an option."

They scribbled down ideas at such a rate that it was like something they did often. Ryan invited Billy to read out his top three.

1. Remove the clothes and burn them. Cut the body into small pieces and scatter it across the course and surrounding area.
2. Return under cover of darkness and remove the body from the course. Get an Argentine army uniform from somewhere and dress it up before placing it near Goose Green.
3. Kill a local resident, bring the body here and make it look like they fought to the death in a golfing dispute.

He knew number three on his list was a non-starter because Ryan would have to forfeit the clubs he had just found.

"OK, I have your number two on my list, so we go with that. I also know where there are loads of rotting Argentine uniforms stored. By the way, number one?"

"The benefits of sharing a cell with Razor McGurk a few years back."

Early afternoon, under cover of darkness, Ryan picked Billy up in his Land Rover. "I've got a uniform, he's going to be a conscript I'm afraid but I figured that would lend him greater anonymity. I mean if a General turns up it might create a bit of publicity."

"Good thinking Ryan. If you don't mind me saying so you seem pretty good at dumping dead bodies."

"We lost a shift driver in '77 when an oxygen bottle blew. It wasn't worth the paperwork so Andrew and I dealt with it ourselves."

That, to Billy was the sort of confession you would make just before you killed the person you had just put in the know. It occurred to him that Ryan was a bit scary.

They collected the body from the fourth and loaded it in the back of Ryan's Land Rover. Half way to Goose Green the unthinkable happened, they were followed then pulled over by Constable Caulton, out doing his sheep protection rounds.

"My, my, it's Billy Hunt," he smiled as he leaned in the passenger window.

Over to you thought Billy, looking at Ryan. I hope you're as good at the old dumping dead bodies thing as you claim to be, if not you and me are in the shit my friend.

"He hijacked my vehicle Constable and put a dead body in the back. He is making me go to Goose Green to dump it. I think it's the tourist you are looking for."

Constable Caulton thought for a moment which for him meant about 5 minutes. He knew there was no dead tourist; they knew there was no dead tourist. They were making a fool of him. He wasn't going to play their silly games and look in the back for what everyone knew didn't exist. "Go on lads, on your way. One day though, Billy Hunt, one day you will slip up and when you do we'll be ready to catch you."

Billy, went over this situation in his mind. He weighed up Ryan's words and reaction, looking from every angle. He could not make his mind up but before he could say anything, Ryan jumped in.

"Look at it this way Billy, you were within an inch of a 20-year stretch, now you are on your way to staying happy and free. In ten minutes another Argie bites the dust on a lonely, soulless hillside. Am I good or am I good?"

"You're good Ryan, you are definitely good."

Billy settled back two nights later for his highlight of the fortnight.

"We have much to report in our news roundup tonight. Missing man Gregory Caulton has been found but unfortunately not in circumstances he or his family wished for. Mr Caulton who had been suffering from a terminal illness had left his home last Tuesday to go to his favourite spot, near the fourth hole on Stanley golf course. As his health deteriorated and he grew closer to death, Mr Caulton had expressed a wish to pass to the other side in this location, where he had first met Mrs Caulton, and where he had scattered her ashes after her untimely death. Each week he would go to his place of prayer to see if the Lord was ready for him yet. After his daughter reported him missing, the family converged on the spot, late Thursday morning, but Mr Caulton could not be found. His golf clubs, a present from his late wife, which he always took to 'show' her, were also missing. It is assumed that young Toby Caulton, stole the golf clubs before removing then dressing up Mr Caulton's body and dumping it at Goose Green. The family are distraught that their relative, a war hero, should be found in the uniform of his sworn enemy. In a statement, the police revealed that they had no evidence of young Toby's involvement in this despicable act but would get something together in due course."

Oops.

Chapter 13

The Supergun

Nightshift, February 1991. TV having at last arrived in the islands, the 'in crowd' had settled down to gawp, "The Hit Man and Her" and all was well on Fantasy Island. Bill Foster was reading his newspaper quietly in the corner of the room. Life was normal, life was adequate, life was just what it was, no more no less.

Then, everything changed.

Bill looked up from his paper, "bet you couldn't build one of these Andrew." He opened the centre page spread and turned the paper towards his colleagues, ensuring that Andrew Williams had an unimpeded view of the headline and picture below. "Iraqi Supergun".

"Piece of cake," lied Andrew. "Give me the objective and I'm on it."

Bill thought for a moment. "The tank farm has thirteen tanks, scattered fairly randomly. I happen to know the greatest distance between any two tanks is that between tank one and tank nine, a distance of half a mile. The objective is to propel a missile of your choosing from east of tank one to land west of tank nine."

"OK," said Andrew before the gauntlet even hit the floor.

Billy went back to the 'hit man', eager not to miss a glimpse of 'her'.

After a relatively quiet shift Billy headed home for a few hours sleep. He got off about 9am having set his alarm for 2pm. At 9:57am he suddenly sat bolt upright in his bed, wide awake in an instant he yelled, "Oh shit!" He found himself sweating and shaking. This sudden awaking was caused by a realisation that they were going to build a supergun of incredible power inside the confines of a bomb of Hiroshima proportions, which was only kept in check by well-maintained equipment, plant and good operations. The great secret to avoiding petrochemical disasters seemed always to focus on one thing, contain the flammable and explosive products as best you can at all times. It was page one of the 'How Not To Blow Up Your Oil Terminal' manual. This advice had only been written in at revision two stage, following a fire at BP Chemicals in Grangemouth caused by a loss of Ethane containment.

He didn't even consider going back to sleep, no point, he would not be able to. He got up and wondered whether he should phone Ryan. He did not want to wake Ryan, who had heard the same exchange he had in the early hours of this morning but he so wanted to hear someone say, "It's OK Billy, this is just not going to happen." Only Ryan would have the sense to say those words. He had to phone him. He phoned.

"Ryan, sorry to wake you, I just had a horrible thought ..."

"Trust me, I haven't been to sleep yet and I know exactly what you are thinking."

"Will we be OK, I mean will we get this stopped or if not will get away with it, fuck it, are we all going to die?"

"Quite possibly. Let me share my thoughts on the matter. Bill foolishly threw down a challenge to Andrew and Andrew foolishly accepted the challenge, stating acceptance before witnesses. On that basis get one thing clear and never doubt this one thing, there is no way this is not going to happen."

"Fuck, shit, I'm scared," whined Billy curling up into the foetal position.

"Me too Billy, but let's think about this. They are doing this thing and we are never going to stop them. So, do we allow it to happen without technical input, you being the only technician among us, and without a restraining voice of reason, that would be me?"

"I take your point. We are in whether we like it or not. We can make them do it safely."

"If you think firing a missile at high velocity within the confines of an Oil and Gas facility can be done safely, maybe you should go back to your market stall. No, it will not be safe but it will be risk managed to the best of our abilities and that's as good as it gets I'm afraid."

Billy felt better, not good, but better at least. Ryan did indeed have a voice of reason and was sensible. He would make this OK, he felt sure.

The first meeting of the 'Project Missile' group was held nine nights after the conception of the idea.

Ryan took the chair as usual, in attendance were Bill Foster, challenger; Andrew Williams, challenged (in every sense of the word); and interested parties, Roddie Ratner, Bobby Mitchell and Billy himself.

Ryan got the ball rolling. "Lads, I would like to start by urging you all to consider the possible implications of the act we are about to embark upon. If anyone has doubts, please speak now."

Nobody spoke, what was the point. This was going to happen.

"OK, Andrew what have you got for us?"

Andrew rose and walked over to a flip chart in the corner of the room. "The challenge we face is to get enough stored energy released onto the back of the yet to be designed missile in a time which will enable maximum forward trust. The release mechanism is the key to everything and it will determine success or failure. The projectile itself needs to be aerodynamic, that goes without saying, and I propose a ball bearing filed to a point. Guidance will be Bill's problem, he may, and I've already discussed this matter with him, require test firings to be made from smaller prototypes of the supergun."

"OK," said Ryan, "it's a good start. Roddie, you will take charge of security, Bobby you will obviously distract attention away from what we are doing, and I think Billy should work on the release mechanism."

Working on the release mechanism gave Billy the idea that he might be able to limit the thrust behind the projectile in a way that would not be obvious to anyone watching. The difference between a modified ball bearing travelling at 1000mph and 50mph was neither here nor there because at either speed you would not actually see it. This project was not about achieving the objective so much as believing you have achieved the objective, Billy had made a career out of such deception. He knew Ryan had given him this key role for that very reason and he slept happier in the locker room that night.

Another meeting was called on the following nightshift. Billy became concerned at the pace the project was being driven forward. He had hoped that time might save them, let the thing go cold was a viable option, but not at this pace.

The first prototype was ready in a week. It was not pretty but it looked functional and could be carried in pockets and assembled at the firing range.

The firing range for the first test was on waste ground far beyond the back of the tank farm. 'Mini Gun' as it was called, was assembled and Billy took the release mechanism out of his pocket. It was just a simple pneumatic solenoid valve. The idea was to attach a nitrogen cylinder, and for test purposes a 1000 pounds per square inch (PSI) one was chosen to the input of the solenoid then connect the output of the solenoid to a four-foot half-inch stainless-steel pipe. A puffer was connected to the gate of the solenoid. At about 15 PSI, easily puffed, the solenoid would open and the 1000 PSI would hit the back of the ball bearing.

The purpose of the test was to examine the projectiles stability in flight, with the intention of learning what shape would enhance flight the most.

With everything assembled and the ball bearing dropped into the pipe, Andrew aimed the pipe toward a wooden fence. Billy puffed and after 25 seconds the solenoid open, the gun fired and the ball bearing dropped to the ground four feet in front of the weapon. People were careful not to point fingers with Roddie present but looks were exchanged and then looks united and focused on Billy.

"I know, I'll work on it," he muttered bowing his head in shame.

A week later the prototype was assembled again and this time a small 50 PSI nitrogen bottle was connected to the gate of the solenoid to enable a snap opening of the pressure path.

When it was fired the ball bearing, which had an extra week's development under its belt went straight though the wooden fence, some 50 yards distant. Things were looking up, or down, depending on your point of view.

A date for the objective firing was set two weeks hence, on a Sunday night shift. During that time the stainless-steel pipe would be looked into, to decide on barrel length. A ball bearing would be prepared and a 6000 PSI nitrogen cylinder would be hidden onsite near tank one.

"How will we actually know if the objective has been achieved," asked Bill.

A good question as it happened because no one would be able to track the missile by sight. They would have to find something beyond tank 9 to aim at, something they could reasonable expect to hit over that distance, something that would show clearly that it had been hit.

Ryan looked at Bill, "Could you hit Billy's shift van over that range?" The answer was yes, it would need to be parked sideways on, 100 feet beyond tank nine and in a direct line with both object tanks. Once again, Ryan the brake had opened the door for Billy.

Later that night after everyone was asleep, Ryan met with Billy in the workshop.

"We are in good shape Billy," he said. Your release mechanism must use only 15 PSI for the gate of the solenoid while appearing to use 50 PSI. You must make a hole in the side of your van the night before we fire, is that all feasible?"

"Not a problem, but what if they see the hole in the van?"

Ryan thought for a moment. "They won't, I will take the van to its position and I'll collect it from the workshop, we don't let that van anywhere near the launch site where they will all be gathered."

The big night arrived and everyone took up position. Ryan radioed a coded message to Andrew which told the firing crew that the van was in place and he was well clear. The supergun was assembled and all component parts were connected. Had Billy concentrated a little more in maths, he might have deduced that opening the solenoid a little slower by using less pressure made not a jot of difference when a fully charged 6000 PSI bottle was used rather than a lower pressure bottle like in the initial test fire. It was all to do with exponential curves, but by the time Miss Lightfoot had got to these, Billy was at 425,000 and was keen to reach his half-million before end of term.

A countdown was performed and then the gun was fired. It was a huge anti-climax in the sense that there was no bang, just a whoosh and a whistling sound as the projectile flew off into the distance. The whistling sound was a concern to Billy as he had hoped to walk forward a few feet and casually place his foot on top of the discharged ball bearing to hide it from view.

Everyone ran to a nearby van and headed for the west side of tank nine. Ryan was there when they arrived, having been given the all clear to move in via the radio. He ran towards them unable to conceal his mock excitement.

"You did it lads, look, see the hole in Billy's van. Everyone congratulated each other and headed back to the launch site to tidy up before day broke.

Billy and Ryan travelled in his van. "I heard whistling Ryan."

"What?"

"When it was fired, the bullet whistled as it would if it were travelling away at high velocity."

"Impossible," said Ryan more in hope than belief. "Look, we'll hang around after they have all gone and we'll find the ball bearing, just for our own peace of mind."

They searched for hours and it was nowhere to be seen. They decided it may have gone further than they hoped, accepted they would never find it and hoped for the best.

It took three weeks for the entire one million barrels of oil in tank nine to discharge into the bund. The time was of greatest significance to the tank farm operators who had to a man, logged the words, "All OK" in their nightshift logs.

The company set aside the nightshift logs for later viewing and focused solely on aspects of how a million barrels of crude oil had liberated itself from the tank.

Once it was established that the missile had hit tank nine, Billy was presented with the problem of explaining to the lads how it had also gone through the side of his van. Billy reminded them of the Kennedy magic bullet theory and for a while the heat subsided, but from that day forward doubts about his credibility would surface with too great a frequency for him to feel comfortable.

While the company never accused anyone of direct involvement in the catastrophe, a short while after it they began to break up 'B' Shift, spreading its members across the other four shifts. Life was never the same again; they had gone too far and wrecked a 'good thing'. Going too far though, was precisely what made him fit. For the only time in his life he had found kindred spirits with a self-destruct button attached to their brains.

For Billy it was the end, he wanted out, he could not bear the boredom of life in the Falklands without his 'B' Shift pals to lift his spirits at work and to cap it all, his golfing buddy was banished to 'A' Shift. What a waste of a 'brake'. 'A' Shift never got out of first gear.

He began looking for work, but decided it would be easier if he were back home in the UK so he resigned and made arrangements to leave as soon as possible.

Chapter 14

Underboss and Weeble

Billy arrived in Portsmouth on 15th August 1992, the fifteenth anniversary of his introduction to working life. He had already decided to mark the anniversary by making this the date which began his non working life—for a while at least anyway.

The fact was, Billy had been earning good money for the last seven years and had spent very little of it. He was a man of means if not substance. As he travelled north he calculated the likely cost of living back in Linlithgow with the purpose of establishing how many years he would not have to work for.

By the time he got home, in the town sense, as opposed to the roof over head sense, because he had nowhere to live, he reckoned about five years of leisure lay ahead of him.

He took a room at the Bonside Lodge, paying for one week, which should give him time to find somewhere to rent or better still share. Out came the contacts book, where were his friends, what were they doing, did they have a spare room?

Bobby Locke was contacted first. Married, two children, another on the way, Ford Granada ...

Gordon Sharp, married to fashion designer, leaving to tour United States with Cindytalk, fourth studio album completed and release imminent ...

Gordon Laird, "Fuck off." Fair enough really, Gordon had been tarred with the brush of fraud and you can't expect that to be forgiven or forgotten, it leaves a stain on your character for life.

He hesitated before calling Lanna Green, took a deep breath and dialled the number.

"Hi, Lanna, sorry I haven't been in touch. How was the divorce for you, are you getting over it yet?" He did sarcasm so well.

"Hey, it's good to hear from you, please tell me this is a long distance call, please."

"No, Lanna, as it happens I'm back in Linlithgow and you are the first person I wanted to call," he lied.

"Let me save you some time Billy, I'm married, have three lovely children and I don't want to see you, far less let you stay in the back room of my house, I assume that's why you are calling, to get digs from me."

The lies were getting easier. "Not at all, just wanted to say hello and see you were OK. So you're married then. Sorted out the whole lesbian thing I assume. Did you get patches to wean you off it or did you have to go 'cold turkey'.

Inexplicably, she hung up and that was it, the end of a beautiful friendship. To this day they have never spoken again.

He continued calling people, none of whom he'd ever bothered to keep in touch with. Some doors were eased closed, others slammed in his face. Everyone had moved on and no one wanted to revisit the past. Maybe mid-life crisis would make them feel differently, but for now, he realised he was on his own.

He was sitting at the Bonside Lodge bar reading the paper a couple of days after his return when a job vacancy jumped off the page, slapped him in the face, then settled back to a destiny of being fading news print. He didn't need or want a job just now but this one interested him.

The vacancy was "Instrument Technician required. The successful applicant will be a member of a highly-skilled team and duties will include planned maintenance and ad hoc remedial works as required."

He was struck by the simplicity of it. It was such a 'we need a warm body, please come soon,' kind of advert. No not an advert, it was an appeal. He was also struck by the fact the vacancy was on Skye, a beautiful Scottish Island which was so close to the west coast of Scotland, he had read somewhere they might even bridge the gap.

There was no comparison between Islands 8000 miles away from Scotland and Islands so close it is feasible to join them to the Scottish Mainland by road bridge. From this place you could 'nip' home. The advantage of applying for island jobs was that nobody else wanted them, so you stood a chance. He decided on impulse to phone off for an application form and information pack.

Two days later he had read his information pack, fallen in love with Skye and posted a completed application. A further two days passed before he found himself seated in the presence of Robert McDonald an Instrument Supervisor and David Wilkes, a twat.

The interview went very well; he knew from the start that McDonald wanted him while Wilkes favoured the other candidate, a local entry. This was a simple case of 'we should take the better suited man' against, 'we should take the cheapest option'. Technical benefit won the day and Billy was soon in the employ of Fina at Soay Oil Terminal.

The progression to being the 'better man' was not lost on Billy and he felt quite proud, until he later met the 'cheaper option' who turned out to have only one leg and held the intellectual capacity of a damp fence post. Still, the better man he was and this was progress indeed.

Hindu Prince Gautama Siddharta, the founder of Buddhism had said, 'To conquer oneself is greater than to conquer others." Billy Hunt said, 'Look after number one." All he knew was, he was going to Skye to get richer and Buddhists lived on a daily ration of peace, gratitude, wisdom and compassion, none of which led to a comfortable retirement in a top floor flat on Gorgie Road in Edinburgh overlooking Tynecastle, the home of Heart of Midlothian Football Club.

Seven years on Skye would buy the dream, he accepted the job and packed his bags.

Fina had a different slant on relocation, whereas BP adopted an arrive, sit down put your feet up policy, Fina took the more pragmatic, 'You're on your own boy" attitude.

The oil terminal itself was not on mainland Skye but on the small island of Soay, a 20-minute twice-daily boat ride away. Soay did not stretch to housing so the boat ride was compulsory. Billy rented a small two-bedroomed house in Torrin, a short drive from the Soay Pier.

He presented himself at the gatehouse on his first day and was taken directly to Robert McDonald's office. He was given an induction sheet which represented a far more sensible approach to the matter than he had previously experienced. The paper simply had a list of appointments for the day. In all he had four meetings arranged with managers from Process Area, Offsites Area, Power House and Engineering. He was told that each meeting would just be a chat about terminal life and he was encouraged to talk as much as he listened.

Meeting One—Process.

Billy was led into the office of Matt Peters, a rotund, obnoxious Welshman. Peters was loud, brash, extremely stupid and had absolutely no desire to take part in a cosy little chat with the commodity he would call upon as a last resort and then stand over with a stop watch.

Meeting Two—Offsites

John Pinkfish stood with an out stretched hand as he entered the office. Billy was asked to make himself comfortable while his host went to make him coffee and once both men were seated with refreshments, a two-hour exchange of words flowed freely. Talking and listening were given equal time. Pauses were in no way awkward and photographs showing John's racing cars were pored over. Billy had never met a more pleasant man and this frightened him. He had managed to get through industry thus far by treating his supervisors with contempt, how do you live with letting down a guy this nice.

Shutdown Matt's plant, fuck him, shut down John's plant, guilt and remorse. It may be that this was the time and place that the seed of a conscience began germinating in Billy's brain. A quick termination was called for.

Meeting Three—Power House

Mick Gray soon brought Billy back to the industry he knew and loved. An arrogant man who despised technicians and anyone else who had an education and a qualification to prove it. He was the stereotypical ditch digger made good, doubtless through endurance and many years of service, before being finally promoted to enhance a pension as reward for stickability and loyalty to everyone above and no one below. Billy didn't listen to a word of his self-praise or his pompous outbursts which coincided with the event of anyone moving within earshot of his door. This was more like it.

Meeting Four—Engineering

This was the meeting that mattered most because he would meet the man who would one day sack him, and learning how this man thought may serve to delay that day.

Billy knocked, waited, then entered the office after invitation; he was immediately put off guard by the sight of Ronnie Biggs sitting behind Terry Norton's desk. OK, it had to be Terry Norton as advertised on the door but this guy was a ringer for the train robber.

Coffee was not offered and Billy was asked to sit a moment while his host finished marking up some papers in front of him. This man made him feel nervous and uncomfortable. After what seemed an eternity the papers were turned over, moved to one side and Norton looked up at Billy. He looked as uncomfortable as Billy felt. This was not a touchy feely human being; this was a cold and dispassionate man.

"Welcome to Soay Billy," unexpected. "We have accrued over 28,000 hours since our last LTA," confusing. "Are you an LTA about to happen Billy?" eh?

Billy thought for too long but finally realised LTA meant 'Lost Time Accident', any injury which was recorded as having caused the injured party to be absent from duty due to that injury.

"No Mr Norton, I do not believe I am. In fact I can tell you I have never been the victim of a recorded injury."

The train robber smiled, a most unexpected and disquieting smile. Some people are not built to smile and Norton certainly fitted this category.

"You have oil terminal experience I see. This is good. What does RoSPA stand for Mr Hunt?"

Billy always remembered a story his father had told him about his national service. He had been on a boat headed for South Korea and was spending a rare day on deck as opposed to having his head in a toilet pan being sick. The men had been lined up and an Officer walked down the line before stopping at his father. "How many portholes on the starboard side soldier?"

"Thirty-seven sir."

The officer nodded and moved on. Thirty seven might have been right but the chances were slim. The point was, his father had answered quickly and positively and the actual number he said did not matter because the officer did not know. Had he paused or admitted not knowing the officer would not have given him the answer he would have scolded him and sent him to count them. Power is not a measurement from a static line, it is the measurement of a gap, the gap between one person's perceived might and another's perceived lack of might.

"Royal Ornithology Society Persons Association." There could in theory be 37 port holes on the starboard side of a troop ship, unlikely but possible; it was as good a guess as any. Numbers are easy but words are a different matter because they have the potential to sound ridiculous if they are all the wrong ones in the wrong order.

The look on Norton's face probably resembled the last thing the driver saw before being 'coshed'.

"The Royal Society for the Prevention of Accidents."

"Oh, that RoSPA, sorry."

"That will be the first and last time you use bullshit on this oil terminal, are we clear about that?"

No we are fucking not clear about that, thought Billy. That's like Errol Flynn making a movie without a sword. I will not be disarmed before lunch on my first day in my new job. Billy Hunt would not be sitting before you now without having bullshit in his armoury; he would be a failure and a waster. Fina employed me, bullshit and all, deal with it Ronnie. Then he stopped thinking because he worried he might say the words out loud.

"Safety is taken very seriously here. It is paramount and it determines everything we do and how we do it. When you work professionally, responsibly and with skill, safety is important. You are a human being though and one or more of these qualities may lapse, and when it does, safety is no longer important, it is vital. We don't make the effort to be safe, we are safe by nature and instinct; understand?"

Billy understood. He understood that safety was a culture verging on paranoia here and bullshit was an unwelcome house guest. This could only end in tears. The unemployed Brazilian beach bum was on a planet Billy had no desire to visit.

He left the office and headed downstairs to the Instrument Workshop filled with foreboding. Having met Dopey, Happy, Doc and Grumpy, he wondered how he would fare with Sneezy, Bashful and Sleepy, who would doubtless be waiting there to complete his set.

The only technician in residence when he arrived introduced himself as Thomas Roberts. He seemed friendly if a little serious. He asked Billy about his life in The Falklands, Billy told him it was fine. He asked how it compared to Skye; Billy told him it was early days. Roberts insisted that Skye was better, Billy told him that was nice to hear. He then told Billy that if he hated Skye so much he should just fuck off back to the Falklands.

Billy was proud to be a Black Bitch, a person from Linlithgow and he was all for pride in your place of origin, but this guy struck him as being a dangerous insecure lunatic. He made the effort to assure Thomas that he had meant no disrespect and he was sure Skye would be much better than the Falklands, but by this time had lost his new friend's attention. Thomas went back to safely putting 2mm nuts onto 2mm bolts having donned welder's mittens complete with built in steel fingertips.

Lunchtime was still an hour away but already Billy knew this was not a place of work, but the set of a horror movie. He asked Thomas if he could sit anywhere and was told he could sit in the far corner of the workshop at the southernmost bench in the workshop, though it was probably 8000 miles too far north for his liking. Mental note, Thomas Roberts is easily upset and reconciliation is not in his repertoire.

He was at one with his thoughts when suddenly the workshop door flew open and the walls shook. His first instinct was, explosion, but then he saw that a short round body resembling a weeble had entered stage left and was heading straight towards the bench of Thomas Roberts. "Alright ya pinhead fuck."

"What does that even mean Collins?" enquired Roberts angrily, while looking down and around on his bench for a fallen nut.

"Look at you, with your gloves on. Look at you, well just look at you." Billy decided that what this interesting young specimen lacked in the range of vocabulary he made up for through repetition of the few words that he knew. He possessed the mannerisms of an apprentice, testing his status in a man's world. The aggressive over confidence was a shield behind which hid a nervous, scared, insecure young boy.

Thomas found his nut and continued his work, "The new guy has arrived," he said, moving his head south to indicate Billy's position.

Collins, who later became known as Lou Collins did not look over, in fact he consciously did everything to avoid connecting eyes with the 'new guy'. He picked up and put down items of no relevance to his situation, he generally fiddled to keep his mind from the thought of an introduction to a stranger.

It was getting close to lunchtime, so bodies began appearing in dribs and drabs. A very tall, very serious looking lad, about his age, walked in and sat down without speaking to anyone. A limping wise-looking man in his late forties arrived and took up residence in a small room which seemed to be a sub-workshop. A farm labourer meandered in with an air of confidence and dispassionate casualness. Then an actor arrived. An actor? Perhaps an unusual tag to attach to the smart, smooth, smiling man who had entered, but this guy looked like he had come straight from the set of a James Bond shoot. He was cool. Billy didn't know him from Adam but by fuck he was cool, suave too. He walked with control, with purpose and with authority.

The 'actor', unlike the others, did not ignore Billy, instead he headed straight for him and delivered his line. "Rob Cross, you must be Billy. Welcome aboard, are you settling in, do you need anything?"

For the first time that morning Billy relaxed, his existence had been acknowledged and welcomed. "Could you introduce me to everyone please," he whispered.

"Certainly, Billy, sorry if my colleagues have been a little rude, let's do the rounds."

As they headed towards Thomas Roberts, Billy pointed out that he had already spoken with him. They slid smoothly to the left and came upon the weeble. "This is our apprentice Lou Collins, he's a good lad, a bit shy with strangers though aren't you Lou?"

Lou reinforced Rob's appraisal of him by looking down and not speaking.

They moved along to the tall silent lad, "This is Micky Ruddock, he came up through the system here, one of our own products." Micky shook hands and mumbled something inaudible but not hostile. The hostility would develop over time.

"Norbert Lane, he's on shift but the shift men have a bench in the workshop here and tend to mix with us when on days." He was another who looked Billy's age—so at least the squad was largely of the same age group, and that might lead to common interests developing as they got to know him.

Norbert really did look as if he'd just come down from the top field. Billy knew that every team had a bit of a retard and in this case Norbert was him. Never judge a book by the cover would have been useful advice at this point but Billy never thought of that.

Finally Billy was led towards the sub-office, but before entering Rob stopped for a 'word'. "You may have noticed David, who lives in here, limping; we don't talk about the limp. We especially don't talk about it on days he doesn't have it because that means he has an appointment pending to have his leg relimped."

As well as the lines had been delivered, they were wasted on Billy, he hadn't go a clue what the actor was talking about.

Surprisingly, Rob knocked and waited to be invited in before entering. "Sorry to bother you, David Early, this is Billy Hunt, who joined us today."

David Early was as it turned out a very much more pleasant man than any he had met that day—with the exception of John Pinkfish. He asked if Billy was settling in, he told Billy to speak to him if he needed anything and he did this throughout a series of interruptions from instrument technicians who knocked at his door to ask permission to do something. "Can I take the van for five minutes?" Then, "Can I use the air blower?" The series of requests which seemed not to need permission was almost endless.

He assumed David was the supervisor of this crew, he had his own room, he had his own executive chair and no one seemed to do anything without his say so. He wasn't though; Billy knew he was a technician, like the rest of them. It then dawned on him that David filled an industry position which had become out of date and discarded long before he had entered the fray in 1977. David was the power, the Sage, the font of wisdom and guidance. He was an 'Underboss', far more powerful than a boss and far more dangerous. He couldn't sack you, he could make you suffer, and that was much worse.

Billy having earlier realised he was in a horror movie, now decided this one had twists. In fact this was a 1940s gangster horror movie. Modern productions of the genre would show a head being chopped off, the 1940s version leaves it to your imagination, and an imagination takes a real situation to a more frightening level altogether.

Billy thought back to his schooldays, when he would be standing in the playground and someone would just walk up and punch him in the face. Not just teachers either, pupils would do it too. It would be a case of, ouch, right what's for dinner today. Problems that have happened are no longer problems. No, a far worse scenario was when someone walked up to him and said, "I'm going to get you," then walked away. Get him where? Get him how? Get him when? Too many unknowns left to ponder and worry about. This was real terror and Soay's collection of independent misfits clearly favoured this format.

Chapter 15

Joining the Dots

During his first weeks at Soay, he was largely ignored and shunned by his new colleagues, and this suited him fine. He used the time to appraise them. What made each person tick, what was their function within the team, what was their perception of those around them, what did they want to get, what were they willing to give?

A lot of questions, but the answers would hold the key to survival. First, and perhaps most alarmingly, he realised this group had no team dynamic. They were self contained, stand alone entities. This led him to correctly discover that through poor management or a lack of an adequate training budget, each was an expert in his own field. David, Fire and Gas detection; Micky, Emergency Shutdown Systems; Rob, planning, paperwork and Hot Oil Distribution. Norbert, he wasn't sure about because he had not been on days again since they first met, but as he was a retard it was safe to assume he just worked on Pressure Gauges or something similarly simple. His theory did however fail when it came to Thomas Roberts.

It became apparent that Thomas Roberts had somehow bucked the trend and managed to become a well-balanced, good all rounder. He could do everything adequately, if not expertly. He was the nourishing meal of meat, potatoes and two veg. Not as titillating as the lovely lemon sorbet pudding but a beautiful sweet does not hit the spot if not preceded by a good, well-balanced, if unexciting, meal. Thomas was also the glue that bonded this fragile team together, remove him and it would all soon unravel. The company had therefore made the cardinal error of making someone indispensable—worse, he knew it and by fuck did he play it well.

Taking that aside, Thomas was an over confident, moody, arrogant person who belittled him at every opportunity; Billy however, decided that this man was his only hope of actually learning something about the oil terminal's workings, nuances and ways. There was no way that a 'specialist' was going to share self-preserving knowledge with him. His only hope was to become an 'all rounder' and in doing so make himself ready for when a specialist left or died or better still, some new equipment arrived that no one knew anything about.

Thomas, did not like Billy, and this would clearly hinder the flow of knowledge Billy needed to happen. He did know how to change this though, it would not make them close friends but it would earn him the right to exist with luck. Billy forgot about learning Soay systems and redirected his focus to learning about Skye. He learned the population was 9227 at last count, he read about the climate and the place's history. He became an authority on Skye and he began singing the island's praises within earshot of Thomas Roberts.

It soon worked, and Thomas became friendlier. He was, it seemed, happy to work with Billy and he did not appear to have a problem imparting knowledge on a look-and-listen basis. Billy had hoped for a bit of 'hands on' but it was made very clear this was not going to happen. When two instrument technicians calibrate a pressure transmitter the obvious, and indeed normal method is one outside pumping the instrument to an agreed pressure, the other inside checking the corresponding reading on a panel instrument. Not the way Robert Thomas did things. He would pump it up, leave Billy with hands in pockets, walk to the control room, sometimes a distance away, check the reading, then walk back out. By the time Thomas reached the control room the pressure had leaked away a bit giving the impression of a lower reading inside than what he had left outside. No matter, Thomas was happier to play fast and loose with tolerances than to trust Billy on the pump. The man was incapable of trust.

As he watched Thomas and learned, he also began to study the strange and fascinating instrument team dynamic at Soay.

When studying a group it is best to focus first on the least stable member, and if that member happened to be the youngest, all the better, from small acorns had grown these trees. Lou the weeble became the object of his amateur psychology. Lou had, after about a month, become more comfortable in Billy's presence, swearing at him, hitting him and stealing his possessions. Billy rightly took this to be a sign of progress and felt he was slipping into gear and would, in the not too distant future, be coasting in harmony with his colleagues. He knew that silent Micky and retarded Norbert were products of a Soay apprenticeship. He deduced from this that the process of selection and training must be pretty hit or miss. Micky may be quiet but he was a very highly motivated and gifted instrument technician. Norbert was a retarded farmer. Had they been so different from each other on their first day with Fina or had the system made them diverge. What would Lou become? What had he started out as when they got their claws into him? At present he was a wee boy in a man's body, full of fun and mischief. He would be a tradesman in less than a year; could rough edges be chipped off to reveal the gem by that time?

With a normal apprenticeship you start at a dot on day one, aim for a predefined dot at the end of year four and simply join all the dots that fall between the two. Apprenticeships really are that basic.

A few days after starting his study of Lou the two of them found themselves walking up the road from a gas plant towards the workshop. To their right and far below them was a water treatment area. A crash barrier separated the road from the steep banking that led down to this, dirtier, smellier and less desirable area of the Terminal.

Billy decided to get Lou to open up a bit. "Where do you think you'll be in five years Lou?"

While rolling down the hill towards a full water treatment tank Billy realised he had been thrown over the barrier, but that knowledge would form part of a later analysis, right now he had to figure out a way to stop before he splashed and drowned. He'd had his hands in his pockets when launched and that had promoted gathering pace to this point. He now took them out in a bid to use them as brakes somehow. Fortunately he was not properly aligned with the tank at take off and came to a stop in an oily puddle.

What had possessed him to analyse Lou through the avenue of communication? No, think, this would be done by observation alone in Lou's case, others who lay on his couch may be engaged in a meaningful exchange of words but you can't use a one-size-fits-all approach with these fucking lunatics.

Lou he noticed was always uncomfortable in the presence of authority or strangers. Strangers who held authority almost caused apoplexy in him and he would become unable to speak anything more than a few words of gibberish. From this Billy deduced that he was an insecure boy who in the company of those he knew well would overcome his insecurity by becoming a larger-than-life focus of attention. He knew of no name for the condition, so he decided to call it 'weeblism'. In the interests of self-preservation he decided against a course of treatment for Lou at this stage. He also felt time would bring maturity into the equation and this may introduce a level of control to the more dangerous elements of 'weeblism'.

He decided to move on to Micky next because despite having shared less than three words of communication with him in as many months, he was fascinated by Micky. He actually admired his quiet, thoughtful and careful demeanour. Micky had something about him, and the air of mystery added to Billy's fascination.

The entire team had gone for a night out to celebrate an electrical technician being overcome by fumes while carrying out planned maintenance. The electrician had not died but his painting days were behind him and that closed all the doors at Soay. After a good night and too much drink Billy and Micky were left alone at the bar. They chatted, they drank some more and they eventually ended up going back to Micky's house for a nightcap. Billy left at 5am and with his hand on his heart could say it was the best night he'd had in ages. Micky liked all the same music, he liked the same films, in fact they had everything in common. He was great company and once he got talking, a never ending flow of interesting words came out of him. Whatever else happened, at least Billy now had a friend.

After the weekend was over Billy headed for work and then headed straight for Micky's workbench to talk about Nirvana. Mumble, mumble and no eye contact was his greeting. Micky was two different people, and work-Micky was nobody's friend. Again the condition tag was unknown to him so he decided on 'Budgism' to reflect the shifting of the victim's mood from pole to pole.

Billy was disheartened, yes he had created two new terms for the medical dictionaries but he was not actually curing or even understanding his patients. Never a man to give up, Billy broke with the norm and gave up. It was as much the prospect of analysing a retarded farmer as his two failures that led him to draw a line under this project. He decided not to understand the people but to understand the system. This had worked for him at college and it would work for him as an actor in this gangster/horror movie.

The system is, you specialise, each of the Terminal's vital systems had a specialist in place, with one man, Thomas Roberts, floating. The company was putting in an Oil Movements Metering System and this would need a specialist. Who would they choose? They seemed to have no one available, unless of course Roberts wanted to dedicate to single topic. Unlikely, he liked his floating role and the security it brought. In fact, Billy didn't even need to ask, he was told. Terry Norton called him in, reminded him to continue working safely and gave him fiscal metering.

There was no evidence of jealousy or hard feelings, nobody wanted metering. Every part of the oil terminal was overhead until metered oil slipped through a jetty valve and fell into an oil tanker's bowels. It was the shop keeper's counter. The point at which all the stuff on the shop keeper's side was balanced off against payment by the customer. Get this wrong and there was nowhere to run, this was fiscal and fiscal errors lead to a damp cell.

Billy thought of it more as a challenge than a road to jail and he threw himself into fiscal metering with great enthusiasm.

If the operational side of fiscal metering went wrong he would have John Pinkfish for a cell mate. He could handle that, he was a good guy and more importantly was happily married and straight as a dye.

Soon after embarking on a meaningful role at the Terminal, Billy learned that specialising brought rewards. Within two weeks he was sent to Haydock, near Manchester, to learn the workings of Maxi-Vis. He correctly assumed that 'Maxi' meant maximum and 'Vis' related to the visual aspects of the machine. He probably didn't need a course, having figured most of it out for himself, but he went anyway.

TCS, the Maxi-Vis people, decided that when teaching a complex subject from the bottom up, it was best to put Penny Parker in as tutor. Penny was tall, slim, blond and beautiful. This immediately called into question, TCS's ability to train its customers as Billy just spent three days looking at Penny and ignored the big cubicle in the corner of the room, inside which sat Maxi-Vis. Another way to look at it was that if their end users could not learn Maxi-Vis, a lucrative support contact would be purchased from them. Either way, Penny was great.

On the flight home Billy looked at his three page Maxi-Vis manual. It turned out that Maxi-Vis was a computer. Its purpose was to receive raw inputs from less intelligent sources and manipulate them in order to provide calculated, accurate and recordable figures. He was struck by how far computers had moved on, from a tiny little ZX81 to a computer which took up a large cubicle, progress indeed. If computers kept getting bigger, where would it all end?

Ironically Maxi-Vis was based largely on maths and like maths was something he would never need to know, because others did it and they would help him.

Billy had an empire and he had Maxi-Vis to run it. What could possibly go wrong?

Chapter 16

When Is A Pint Not A Pint?

Measuring quantities of oil was a much more complex pastime than Billy could ever have imagined. When they put a computer in charge, he should have realised that fact, but he didn't. Basically if you took a pint of oil from beneath the Atlantic Ocean, processed it, removing the bits that aren't really oil, then stored it, then moved it to a big boat, what you ended up with was not a pint. The only part fiscal metering concerned itself with was the quantity that left the onshore tank and the quantity that arrived on the tanker. This, thought Billy, would significantly simplify his role in proceedings, but he was wrong.

The oil put onto the boat would be at a different pressure and temperature, possibly even density than that which left the storage tank; this meant a pint was not a pint. The difference in quantity if the product was beer would not start a bar room brawl, but where oil was concerned the difference made lawyers richer. The customer wasn't keen to pay for what you said he was getting and favoured paying for what he actually got. Billy could understand this, having been a market trader.

"Have you got Return to Fantasy by Uriah Heep?"

"Yes, it's £1."

"OK, I'll take it. Wait a minute, it has no cover and the record is scratched."

"OK, call it 60p."

Selling crude oil was exactly the same as selling records and as long as Billy remembered this he was sure he would be fine.

His main function was to check the calibration of the instruments which threw all the important information at Maxi-Vis. You couldn't simply apply a pressure to a pressure transmitter and check the reading was OK though. This was fiscal metering; it had to be a bit more technical than that. The applied pressure needed to be manipulated; factors had to be factored in, phase of the moon and tide times recorded for auditors to review.

A typical example of this approach to selling oil was the calibration of a simple pressure transmitter.

First you had to use expensive and certified instruments to apply the pressure then measure the readings in the control room. So Billy would get Lou to go outside and apply 10 BarG to the instrument. In normal circumstances he would look at the reading inside and see if it was near enough 10 BarG. In the world of fiscal metering the pressure he needed to see might be in the region of 10.044 BarG. This was because the following formula had to be applied to the original pressure, take a deep breath:

(Local Gravity / Standard Gravity) * Applied Pressure + (0.002 * (20 – Dead Weight Tester Temperature) / 100 * Corrected Pressure) + ((((Static Head – Dead Weight Tester Height Difference) / 10.21) * Nominal Specific Gravity) / 1000)

Remember, this is oil being sold, not diamonds. Interestingly Billy was fully vindicated in his decision 20 years earlier, to ignore equations. He had done so on the assumption that someone clever would do all this for him if he ever needed it done. Someone clever did do it, using something clever, a PC-based spreadsheet.

A company named I.T.E. provided a full set of spreadsheets at great expense, which enabled Billy to just put in one number and within a second or two the answer he was looking for popped up on the screen.

To run the spreadsheets a laptop computer was provided, an old Amstrad 386 with monochrome screen. Lotus 123 provided the magic. All Billy had to do was put a number in box one and watch the spreadsheet run around with it, picking up and manipulating the variables on its way to providing a recordable and possibly meaningful value to show the auditors and lawyers.

And that was where the end began. Billy, having dodged PCs in 1981, was given a second chance to fall under their spell. There was something about pushing numbers on a keyboard and watching impossible things happen on a screen, in real time, which fascinated him. PCs became an obsession and it was not long before he fell out of love with instruments, finding them too simple. As his job title was Instrument Technician, it became a concern to his managers that he would not entertain any job which did not involve the use of a PC.

Around the time Billy fell in love with PCs, Rob Cross had the good fortune to be promoted away from working with hand tools, which were making his hands terribly rough. Unfortunately he had the misfortune to become a planning supervisor. His new role put him at odds with Billy, because his role was to maximise completion of planned maintenance works using the limited amount of human resources at his disposal. When one fifth of your human resources suddenly decides he will only work on the very limited number of tasks which involve a PC, you have a serious problem.

This was initially tackled in a spirit of mutual respect and a desire not to fall out, as they had become quite good friends by this time. The two men sat down and found ways to accommodate each other's wishes. It was decided for example that Billy could make up a small spreadsheet to record pressure gauge calibrations, completely unnecessary but it seemed a good compromise and at least this led to pressure gauges being calibrated with great enthusiasm. Despite their best efforts to involve PCs in many aspects of the instrument team's work, they had not spotted an obvious problem. No one else, with the one exception of Lou Collins, wanted to use PCs, so they shied away from work that was converted or adapted to use a laptop.

Lou had become interested, but unlike Billy, not obsessed with PCs, because Billy had decided from the outset that he needed someone to assist him with running the Fiscal Metering empire. The golden rule of being a specialist is, never tell anyone what you are doing and how you are doing it. In this case Billy had little choice, he could not be outside in the wind and rain pumping up a pressure transmitter and at the same time be inside drinking coffee and smoking a cigarette while taking the readings. Quite simply he needed another pair of hands and Lou's hands were available at the time.

Lou was perfect. Shortly after they had cashed the cheque, I.T.E.'s Lotus spreadsheets became obsolete and a need arose to update them all, numbering nearly 100, to work with Microsoft Excel. This presented Billy with two problems: first he didn't know how to do it, and second he didn't want to do it. Lou took on the task and made short work of producing better looking, quicker calculating and more user-friendly spreadsheets. Lou's lack of communication skills meant he could not tell management how clever he was and this enabled Billy to take all the credit for the good work that had been done. He even received a tidy sum of money by way of a bonus.

Things were going particularly well and that was a state which seldom remained constant in the life of Billy Hunt. True to the script, at the peak of his powers, problems began to arise at an alarming rate.

He had completely forgotten to consult the underboss while growing his empire and this led to rising tensions in the workshop. Billy decided that his best plan would be to enter into a power struggle.

In the Red Corner the incomer, versus, in the Blue Corner, the man born and bred in Skye who had over 25 years of unblemished service as a solid citizen on Soay Terminal. Billy was confident. After a few early rounds of 'my dad's bigger than your dad' it became apparent that the ongoing skirmish may ultimately lead to more physical confrontations, so having Lou on his side would help. As insurance Billy decided to also recruit Norbert the retard into his band of merry men.

Towards the end of 1998 Billy invited the two men into an office he had taken to squatting in over in the Offsites building. Both were late for the meeting because like everyone else on the Terminal they were unaware that he even had an office, never mind where it was. Having eventually tracked him down they were invited in and seated on a couple of stools while Billy reclined in a leather office-chair.

He was confident he would get Lou on board because of his involvement in fiscal metering in the past two years.

Norbert the retard was a different kettle of fish entirely, simply because Billy had made a very small error of judgement very soon after first meeting Norbert. His first impression of Norbert had been, 'farmer' and it was true he was a farmer. His decision to add the tag retard to Norbert's name was based on the fact that those with farming connections at Solheim Inlet had all been particularly stupid. Unfortunately he had not realised that Norbert was and still is the most skilled and gifted man in industry, and we are not talking local industry or even national industry here. It would be fair to say that Norbert is in fact the cleverest man alive, in the World. That on all levels makes 'Norbert the Retard' a bad name. But what's in a name?

He decided to bring Norbert on board first because he would probably be more difficult. The policy of allowing people to become specialists was a flawed one, but it was continued because people liked being specialists as it was good for job security and pride. The difficulty with Norbert was that he didn't fit into the happy-to-be-good-at-one-thing template, as he was brilliant at everything. His mind needed to be constantly challenged and stretched or he just got bored and started crashing vans.

"How do you feel about the greater use of PCs in our day to day work Norbert?"

"Why?"

Billy explained that they made things easier, were better and faster when making up calibration records and were good fun to use.

The problem was of course that Norbert could do everything a PC could do in his head, just a bit quicker. He was a non-starter and in fact became hostile towards Billy's plans for Soay domination on the grounds that he was a socialist and a good guy who liked fairness across the board. He looked at Billy and spotted a guy who given an inch would take a mile.

Turning to Lou, "What do you think Lou?"

He had expected a grateful grunt of accession at this point and nearly sat up in his swivel chair when Lou presented him with a typed up document with a cover title of 'Collins Theory of Expansion'.

How had this obnoxious, semi-literate thug turned into someone who could suddenly put a coherent case for the meeting of his desires into a written document with a leather bound cover which even had his own logo on it. What the fuck had occurred here while the new Compaq 486 laptop had been diverting his eye from the ball. Billy was the victim of Lou grasping the opportunity everyone thought he'd been kind in giving to him, when in fact he just wanted someone to do the shitty outside bit of fiscal metering—particularly when the weather turned cold. For the first time in his life bullshit and illusion had slipped the leash and turned on him to bite mercilessly at the hand which was meant to look like it had food in it.

The demands were so well presented and so ridiculous that Billy was in awe of them. He'd thought he was good at stuff like this, but he was an amateur compared to the weeble.

Out the corner of his eye he saw Norbert smile and suddenly he remembered Lou's own interest in farming albeit not on the same scale as the retard. Billy decided in an instant, if he could have his time again and change only one thing, he would heed the advice given to him by Razor McGurk, the toughest man in Saughton. "Never fuck with farmers Billy."

He could not remember the context or set of circumstances which caused that particular comment to be made in the 'D' Wing showers, he had been far more focused on not dropping his soap. Why hadn't he dropped the soap and listened? It would have been so much less painful in the long run.

Basically when you cut through the prologue, the table of contents, the presentation, the summary and the index at the back, Lou's proposal was pretty straight forward. The 250-page document could be summarised as 'Fuck you, I'm taking over now'.

Billy thanked them both for their time and showed them to the door of Lou's office before closing it behind them and having a massive heart attack.

Fina were fantastic, they sent flowers and a booklet on early retirement. The booklet contained pictures of happy 60-year-old men playing tennis. He flicked through for pictures of happy 40-year-old-men having sex, but was unable to find any. Could he really retire at 40 because that was the non-negotiable offer on the table?

He looked at his savings, he looked at his proposed retirement income, and then he looked at his feet which were blue. Yes he could—and what's more, fuck them all, he would.

Chapter 17

The Window

Having spent the majority of his working life on islands, where disposable income was not easy to get rid of, Billy was quite wealthy.

As a boy his father had taken him to Tynecastle for every home game, to watch Heart of Midlothian battle to break free from years of mediocrity. At half time he would eat his pie, drink his Bovril and speak to his father about all manner of topics. One topic which came up more frequently than any other was the flats on Gorgie Road which overlooked the pitch. He would look up at people sitting at their living room watching the match.

"One day Dad, I will live there."

His father had probably hoped his son would achieve some sort of greatness which would spare him from such a fate.

On his retirement, Billy decided he would make his dream come true. It would make it all worthwhile. Not many small boys clear the bar they set during the age of innocence, when anything is possible but little is achievable. Billy did. He bought the flat of his youthful dreams. He knew of course that the pitch could no longer be seen, since the construction of a new stand. He knew also that one day the site would be a supermarket. None of this mattered.

Billy sat at his window, looked at the back of the Gorgie End Stand and continued his counting, not a bad life.

7,500,001, 7,500,002, 7,500,003 ...

The End

www.ingramcontent.com/pod-product-compliance
Lightning Source LLC
Chambersburg PA
CBHW051808040426
42446CB00007B/570